THE PUNK

THE PUNK

An L.A. Memoir

Claude L. Russell

VANTAGE PRESS
New York

Although based on true events of the author's life, this is a work of fiction. Any similarity between the names and characters in this book and any real persons, living or dead, is purely coincidental.

FIRST EDITION

Published by Vantage Press, Inc.
419 Park Ave. South, New York, NY 10016

Manufactured in the United States of America
ISBN: 978-0-533-15699-3

Library of Congress Catalog Card No.: 2006939187

0 9 8 7 6 5 4 3 2 1

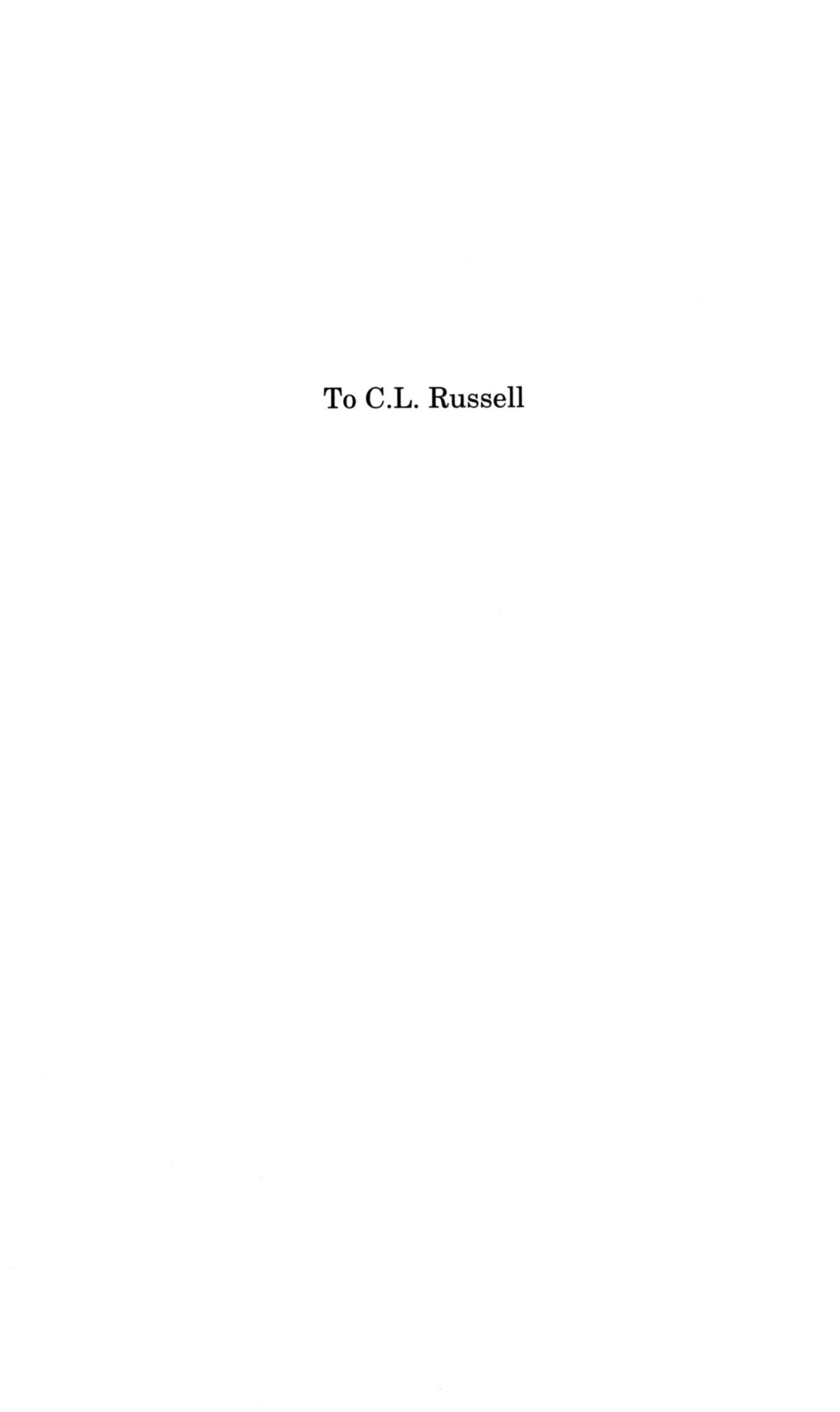

To C.L. Russell

Contents

Foreword

Some years ago when I was living in California, I became enamored of certain memoir accounts of California history and plunged off into a search for material that told how the Golden State came into being by those present at its creation and advancement.

I read books like Richard Henry Dana's *Two Years Before the Mast*, J.S. Holliday's *The World Rushed In*, Kevin Starr's *City on a Hill* and Carey McWilliams's *California: the Great Exception*. But the texts that gripped me the hardest weren't these well-known publications that every serious student of California history has on his bookshelf next to his Hubert Howe Bancroft sixteen volume *History of California*, it was the smaller, more personal texts of California history as experienced by succeeding generations of Californians.

Perhaps this was due to the fact that I was a native Californian who had just acquired some illuminating original documents relating to his family's settlement of a Mexican land grant in central California. That certainly had something to do with it. When I saw a messy, handwritten letter from Captain John Augustus Sutter complaining to my forebear that he was charging Sutter too much for milling grain, it made that storied time all the more personal for me. It was living history, told in an all-too-human voice.

The topic of personal California history became a

guilty pleasure of mine; a private obsession that I didn't share with many. I figured that it would go on this way, and I'd feed my desire for more of it whenever I went back to California, which was periodic since my arrival here in Oregon. I did not expect to find a fount of this kind of personal history in Florence, Oregon, but I sure did.

When I first met Claude Russell in February of 2003, I was about to conclude that initial meeting with a polite decline of his offer to edit and ghost-write his book. I was about to leave his house when the whole of *The Punk: A Memoir of Los Angeles* suddenly took shape. What suggested itself to me was a book that was a memoir of pain and understanding and eventual acceptance.

Russ and I agreed on this and we put together an outline that we intended to follow. I thought it would take us four months or so to write. It took us six. I knew that the ending would be the most difficult part of the book for Russ, and I told him this sometime around April. I told him that I was going to make him work and that he wouldn't like doing some of that work because it could potentially evoke a great deal of pain. Russ said he was ready for this, but I didn't really think he knew how painful it would be. "Believe me, Russ," I told him, "you're not going to like me by the time this book is finished."

Unfortunately, that prophecy proved to be true. Russ didn't want to go to Ensenada, Mexico to see Greg Velasco before he, the man who Russ calls "Papa", died. He didn't like dredging up some of the other painful memories contained herein. He hated the continual questioning from me of how he knew what he knew and what he had to support what he knew; and he hated the process of rewriting and revision. For him, the book was done as soon as he finished the telling of it. For me, that was just the foundation.

This book is entirely Claude Russell's book. All the events describe herein are depicted in Russ' language and terminology. All I did was transcribe those words from the taped interviews I conducted with him and place them in their proper order according to the outline that he and I wrote in February. Some of these opinions and depictions of events in his life became a source of debate for us during the time that we spent working together on *The Punk*. But this is his book, and these are his opinions and conclusions about his life.

From all I can tell, it was at the very least a most interesting life. Certainly, it was one that was worth documenting in a book. Russ survived a chaotic period of dislocation and non-blood-relative upbringing directly after his birth. He endured a strange and severe childhood with his grandparents during the Depression, then had a horrific reunion with his natural mother, whose general cruelty and trouble-making were on par with Pandora.

It was a hard life, but Russ managed to find a way to survive it and triumph over it. He was able to transform the hatred he felt into a love that manifested itself in his first and third marriages and his three children. Russ was successful in business and his life was built on friendships that endured.

People like Claude Russell are almost obsolete now. They are reminders of an American way of life that has nearly vanished; of a time when terms like loyalty, trust, devotion, commitment, and keeping to one's word hadn't yet become the antediluvian artifacts they now are.

We are richer as a people, as a culture, as a nation, for people like Claude Russell, who, almost unwittingly, and to his and our great benefit, kept his unconscious camera of memory winding throughout those years of trauma, trial and outright horror. For this alone, he is to be congratulated.

Like any of us now alive, Russ has challenges ahead of him and things that are not yet resolved to his satisfaction. But whether he still has the time to meet these challenges, some of which he realized during the course of writing this book, is unclear. His Alzheimer's condition is particularly frustrating for him, as is his fragile health. Each day is a different struggle for Russ, and I have seen him at both his best and worst. I pray for his future.

I can truly say that I am a richer person for having known and worked with Claude Russell, the Punk. He brought the early twentieth century Los Angeles alive to me in a way that few other have, and now he had left a record of it. For this alone, we can be grateful. And if this book does help someone else who had to endure a strange and painful series of events such as Claude Russell did, which was his greatest wish to pass on when he finished writing it, then it has been an instructive legacy lesson that he gets to bequeath, similar to the one that "Papa" Greg Velasco bequeathed to him. In my view, that alone is something that is truly and remarkably heroic. The Punk has left us all a worthy legacy.

—Richard Trainor
Eugene, Oregon, September, 2003

Author's Note

The journey through life begins with baby steps. Sometimes these first attempts at locomotion are imprinted in sensitive shifting sand while for others, they are indelibly marked in the hardened mud of a difficult start. Life is a pilgrimage leading down various paths where the answers to nagging questions may be found. *We can make our plans but the final outcome is in God's hands. Proverbs 16:1.*

This story is fictional but based upon real experience. Any disrespect to people, places or organizations is unintentional. It is dedicated to the reality of life and the determination of humanity for survival.

THE PUNK

One
Looking Back from Florence

I now live in a trailer park in a small town on the central Oregon coast where it rains almost every day for six months out of the year. The town is called Florence, an old, played-out fishing town where the Siuslaw river dumps into the Pacific Ocean. It's a pretty and quiet little town of maybe 7,000 people and I've been here for almost six years now.

When I wake up in the mornings I'll hear the rain falling hard on the corrugated tin roof of my trailer. I love that sound that the rain makes on the roof—like pebbles thrown against something hard, like sand being dumped in the back of a dump truck, a sound that I know very well.

When my last wife was alive we used to love to come here in our r.v. We'd drive the hundred and fifty miles from our house out in Quines Creek and spend our time doing the things we enjoyed. We'd go climbing, crabbing, hiking, collecting shells along the beach, and watching the sunset. Then we'd go to dinner or prepare food in the r.v. Then, when my wife BB got terminal cancer, I nursed her for nineteen months and she died in my arms on June 14, 2001. Then I got in a motor home and drove across the country, scattering her ashes in the places she loved, here on the Oregon coast, some in San Diego, and some at her birthplace back in Mississippi.

Sometime during that trip I began to develop the first symptoms of Alzheimer's disease. Then last summer I developed cancer, terminal yet operable, cancer of the blood. So far this year I had a mild heart attack in April and then had a number of tumors removed later in the spring. I know that I'm dying, that there's nothing that can save me short of an outright miracle. I've maybe got a year or so my doctors tell me and the irony of my dying in a town called Florence isn't lost on me because that's where my life began, in a different Florence, a place where it was even more sunny than this place is rainy.

My days here in Florence, Oregon aren't really too eventful or exciting, except if you consider it exciting to be found wandering along the beach not knowing who or where you are. That's happened to me a couple of times here. It's what Alzheimer's does to you. It makes you rummy and you feel like you're in a fog most of the time, and I guess I am.

Like I said before, I usually wake up to the rain beating against the tin roof and when I took outside to the field across from the new high school on 27th Street it's usually gray and misty. Then I'll put on my morning tea, prepare myself a simple and hearty breakfast and sit down to eat it and watch the tube. Lately it's been the war in Iraq and the search for Saddam Hussein and his weapons of mass destruction. I watch it for maybe an hour or so then I feed my orange tabby cat Stumpy. Then I sit, shower, and shave and wait for the time when the local bus stops outside the trailer park so I can run my errands in town.

I usually stop at the Siuslaw Public Library over on Ninth just off Highway 101 and take out some books to read. I like thrillers and suspense novels, current affairs and history, and I'll pick up a few of each. Then I might go across the street to the video store and pick up a movie or two. After that I might walk the other direction and go to the post office if I need stamps. Then when that's all done I'll cross over the highway and go to the Moose Lodge to meet my friends and have a few drinks.

I've been a member of the Moose for almost thirty-five years now—from another time in my life way back when I worked in oil fields and drove semi trucks. Then I was known as "The Punk." They gave me that nickname back when I was a Seabee in World War II serving in the Pacific on places like Guam and Saipan. I didn't earn that name for bad behavior necessarily but because of my age. I was fourteen then but that's a whole other story that we'll get to a little later on.

Like I said, I spend my afternoons at the Moose—usually from one to four. I drink with my friends there and we swap tales of times gone past. With some of the vets here I might talk about the war. With some of the construction guys I might talk about oil rigging or truck driving. My friend Ginger tends the bar and she runs a pretty tight ship. She takes care to see that I get out of here in good shape, sometimes calling a cab for me if she thinks I've had too many. She sees to it that I get home O.K.

When I do get home, I make myself dinner and turn on the tube again and watch some more news. Saddam's on the run, though where he's run to nobody knows. They've blow up many of his palaces though they haven't found his body. There's looting in the streets, calls for the U.N. to take over for the Americans. And so on. After about an hour of this and after I've finished my dinner, I'll go pop a video in the machine. Then at about nine or so I head off to bed taking one of the books that I've picked up at the library.

This winter, sometime in March I think, I picked up a book called *My Dark Places.* It was by a guy named James Ellroy. He's some famous writer and he comes from my home town, though not from the section where I used to live.

In this book, the writer Ellroy is trying to unravel a mystery. It's a murder mystery and the murder victim was Ellroy's mother. She was strangled about fifty years ago. In the end, after about three hundred pages or so, Ellroy doesn't solve the murder; in fact, he doesn't do much throughout the whole book except talk about his miserable childhood in Los Angeles and the hard times he had as a teenager after his mother was killed. He also spends much of the book talking to detectives who worked the case and searching through their old files.

It's all a dead end for Ellroy, he gets nowhere. In the end he doesn't know much more than he did at the beginning, which I thought was kind of sad. For me the book was pretty much a waste of time except for one thing. One character really got to me and that was the murdered mother. She was a redhead. So was my mother. The main difference between Ellroy and me was that he was trying to solve his redheaded mother's murder. The Redhead in my own life was somebody I wanted to kill during the short time I knew her.

Maybe murder is too strong a word for the way that I felt about The Redhead. But I sure felt that way during the time that I spent with her when I was growing up. If that's what you want to call the brief time that we spent together when I was young. But she was absolutely hell on wheels, the Redhead was, and for some reason she took great delight in tormenting me. And I wasn't alone in these feelings that I had toward The Redhead. Nearly everyone who knew her back then felt that way, even her own mother.

As I sit here now thinking about her and the eighteen months or so that I spent with her I wonder how I somehow managed to survive her and the torture she put me through. I wondered how I managed to survive a childhood that was hardly a childhood at all but a period of adulthood lived as a young boy. And the more that I thought about it, the more I thought about Papa.

Papa's not really my papa—not by blood anyway. My real dad was Claude Russell. He was someone I never knew and never really saw. I only heard about him from time to time. The man I called Papa is a man named Gregorio Velasco. Greg's an old man now, ninety-seven, I think. I met Greg in the late 1950's when I was thirty years old. I'm seventy-four now, maybe seventy-six depending on which birth certificate you believe. But that is a whole other story best saved for later.

Papa lives in Ensenada, Mexico with his wife Soccorro. He owned a restaurant there for over fifty years and when I met him back in 1959 I was pretty broken up from a bad truck driving accident. When I arrived there I had my arm in a huge airplane cast. The doctors at Scripps Hospital in San Diego wanted to take the arm off but Papa hooked me up with a brilliant young neurosurgeon who managed to save the arm with a bone-grafting operation that took thirteen hours to perform. The arm took another two years to heal and I spent that time in Ensenada with Greg and his family. It was the second time that Papa saved my life. The first time was when I was just a little baby, which helps explain why I call him Papa.

Although Greg lives in Mexico and is ethnically Hispanic, Papa is also an American who grew up in Los Angeles where his family held a Mexican land grant near what is now Third and Spring Streets. The reason that I call Greg Papa is because that's what he was to me. When I was four months old my parents split up and they left me with Greg and his family. I stayed with them for over three years or so until The Redhead's parents somehow managed to acquire me.

For some reason I had been thinking of Papa a lot this past winter. Maybe it was the fact that I was facing my own mortality that brought it on. Maybe it was Papa's. At ninety-seven I'm sure he's thinking about that. Here I was, in Florence, Oregon, seventy-four or seventy-six with cancer, a bad heart, and an ongoing case of Alzheimer's that clouds much of my memory. There he was, Ensenada, at age ninety-seven, hanging on, surrounded by his family. Between us was eight hundred miles of Pacific coast that I know like the back of my hand.

Through most of the winter I stuck to my usual routine. Breakfasts in front of the tube watching the war, bus into town for the errands, then over to the Moose and back home again. Then one week I had to go over to Eugene, sixty miles away, to see my doctors and have a check-up. I took the Greyhound and stayed in a motel across the street from the station. It was the same story that I'd been hearing for the past couple years—inoperable cancer and certain death sometime soon, probably in the next year or so. By the time I made it back to Florence an idea began to take hold of me.

Actually it was two ideas. I wanted to go see Papa one last time before either of us dies. Who knows which of us will outlast the other? Who knows if he'll still be alive when I get there? Who knows if I'll be able to survive the trip to Ensenada? Who knows? The other idea was to put down on paper what this whole life's journey has been about for me and how Papa played such a large part in my life. Two months ago I picked up a pen and started to unravel this tale as best I could. With Alzheimer's it hasn't been easy.

Sometime during this long rainy winter I began putting the pieces together as best I could. I pulled out old family albums and looked at pictures of Papa and me down in Ensenada and old photos of my own family and the time when I was known as "The Punk." I pulled out old letters and news clippings looking for clues. I took out books from the library with pictures of Los Angeles from the time when I was young and growing up in that part of the city, then know as Florence. And sometime during the same winter I became acquainted with a writer who agreed to help me organize all these pieces into a book.

I met him through a mutual friend in Eugene, who gave him my number. He called me one day and I invited him out to Florence where we could meet. I showed him the family pictures, the old clippings, the books from the library—all the scattered pieces that I'd assembled by then. I had much of this present material recorded on audio tapes and gave it to him to see what he thought. About two weeks later he came back to Florence with the material and said he thought it might work as a book and he agreed to help me put it together. He told me a funny story about a writer who once said that every person had a book in them but that most ought to leave it there. I thought that was pretty good.

What do I know about books? What do I know about literature? What do I know about writing for that matter? The answer is not much. My education, if you want to call it that, ended in 1943 when I was fourteen or sixteen. My background is oil rigging and drilling, truck driving and property maintenance, not literature. How did I know that the one book I possibly had in me wasn't one of those books that was better left there? I didn't.

During one of our conversations this past winter the writer asked me what books I'd been reading lately and I showed him the pile I was wading through. He held up the Ellroy book and asked me what I thought of it. I said that I found it kind of boring, that it was filled with too much detail, that it was mostly about a misspent youth and how Ellroy managed to survive it. But I also told him that the story of the redheaded mother had gotten to me and reminded me of The Redhead that was my mother. Then we talked about Los Angeles and what I remembered of it. He turned on his tape recorder and recorded our conversations. Sometime later, the light went on again and the Alzheimer's fog in my brain began to clear.

I had gone to the Moose one day carrying that book by the L.A. writer and I started to read it again while Ginger poured me a brandy and Coke.

Here's what I thought:

I thought O.K., this guy was thirteen years old when his mother got murdered by who knows who. This was in El Monte, a suburb of Los Angeles not far from the Florence section where I lived as a kid. The murdered mother was a redhead. She catted around—just like my mother did. Then when Ellroy became a famous writer he went back to Los Angeles and tried to figure out who killed her. He flew up and down the state from Los Angeles to Sacramento interviewing retired police detectives and searching through their files. Back and forth he'd fly from the east coast where he lived to the west coast where he grew up assembling the material into a book that grew to over three hundred pages. At the end of it he still wasn't any closer to solving the mystery. I thought, *Why write a mystery book when you can't solve the mystery?* When at the end you're still in the dark as to who did it and who and what your mother really was? That didn't make any sense to me and I told my editor what I thought when I saw him again.

"So you think the book was pretty much a journey to nowhere?" he asked me.

I told him yeah, that I thought it was an interesting story in the beginning but that it ran out of gas after about a hundred pages or so.

"Well how is your book going to be different?" he wanted to know. I told him that I'd have to think about that and would have an answer for him the next time I saw him. We scheduled another meeting for two weeks from then.

During those two weeks that was pretty well all I thought about. The prospect of beginning a book-length journey into the uncharted territory of a very painful past and then arriving at nowhere in particular at the end of it wasn't something I was particularly looking forward to.

Two weeks passed and I still hadn't heard from him. Finally he called me one day to tell me he was back in town. He said he was sorry, that he'd been called out of town on family business. His mother had died unexpectedly and he apologized for being out of touch. I asked him to come out to Florence, and he came over later that week.

During the three weeks that he'd been gone I had been reading many books and putting things down on paper. I'd also made a couple more audio tapes about what I'd been able to remember about those days. One was about the Depression. One was about Grandma and Grandpa. One was all about The Redhead. I remembered all the jobs that I'd had as a kid and listed them on paper.

I'd been a newspaper boy, a potato peeler, a pinsetter in a bowling alley, a small-time bootlegger; you name it, I tried it. You had to in order to survive those hard times back then.

It all seemed like a bad dream back then and it's a wonder to me now that I was able to survive it all. But I think that my ability to get through it was somehow due to the love and care and guidance I was given by Papa and his family during those young formative years that I couldn't even remember. And now, more than anything, I wanted to see Greg one more time to express my gratitude and find out all I could about those unremembered early days. I was determined to do just that. But first I'd have to survive just long enough to make it down to Ensenada.

Two

Depression Days with Grandma and Grandpa

I remember I was blindfolded. There was a moist handkerchief over my eyes and Grandpa was pulling me in my little wagon. I had measles at the time and I guess the handkerchief thing was common treatment for kids back then during the Depression. They said they thought that measles would ruin your eyes if you were exposed to direct sunlight, so Grandma put one on me that day.

We were in a church along Florence Boulevard near where Grandma and Grandpa and I lived. Grandpa worked sometimes at the church as a janitor or night watchman. I forget which. We'd been there for a few minutes or so when suddenly the ground began shaking. I could hear things cracking and other loud sounds of shaking. Then all of a sudden I felt Grandpa push me hard in the back and I went flying across the room in my wagon until it hit a wall. A second later I heard a horrible crashing sound behind me. I pulled off the blindfold to see what was going on.

The giant chandelier that had been right above me just seconds ago was now lying on the church floor. It was smashed to smithereens. The ground shook some more; the roof beams were groaning. The church walls shuddered and whined. It was March 10, 1933. I was almost four years old. The Long Beach earthquake had just struck. It's the first thing I can remember from my childhood and it scared the living hell out of me.

We were living then in a simple frame house at the corner of 67th and Converse Streets, just east of Florence and a little north of Watts, which was then just twelve square blocks or so. Grandma and Grandpa had just gotten me back from the Mexicans then, from Greg and his family. I never did find out how all of that happened and maybe I never will, although I do intend to ask Papa about it when I get down to Ensenada.

Grandma and Grandpa were the Von Strafers. She was Ella and he was Samuel. He was from somewhere back east, from Pennsylvania or Ohio I think. She was from Kansas and this was her second marriage. Her first was to a guy from Texas named Baker and that marriage had produced The Redhead. But I knew nothing about any of that back then and wouldn't learn about it until some years later.

Grandma and Grandpa once had some money and a fair amount of property down in Los Angeles. Then the Great Depression hit, and it hit them pretty hard, but it hit everyone in Los Angeles pretty hard back then.

Grandma was short and chubby, about 5' 1" and 170 pounds or so. She had long gray hair that she swept up on top of her head and tied in a big bun. She wore simple dresses that went all the way down to her ankles and big clunky black shoes. The dresses were usually black or brown or gray. There were no spring colors or fancy prints for her.

Grandma was a tee-totaling, Bible-thumping woman who went to church every day of the week. Sometimes she'd go three times a day and whenever she could she'd drag me along with her. She didn't allow me to play with any of the kids in our neighborhood. She was about as severe as a heart attack when it came to the behavior she allowed. She didn't allow me any leeway, not much, anyway. But she wasn't a mean women, not at all. She was just very strict, very severe and she sure as hell was religious.

Grandpa was a different story. He was taller and leaner, maybe 5' 10" and 180 pounds. He wasn't a Bible-thumper like Grandma was. He was a hard worker and he'd been a carpenter back in his prime. He didn't dress like an undertaker or an Amish man; he liked color and wore it when she'd let him get away with it. He was not a teetotaler.

From that first house we all lived in at 67th and Converse, we moved east less than a year later to another frame house in the Florence section. We stayed there a brief time. Then we picked up and moved again to the big house on 69th and Converse, the one I best remember from my days with the two of them.

From what I've been able to reconstruct of that time in that house right in the heart of the Florence section this is what I've been able to string together.

The house on 69th and Converse was a big single story-house with a basement beneath it and a flight of stairs that led up to the front door. It was battleship gray with full measure 1 X 6 tongue-and-groove shiplap siding. In the front of the house there was a big olive tree and a smaller pepper tree. A big porch ran along the length of the house. The eaves of the house covered the front porch. In the back of the house were a lemon tree and a walnut tree way out by the back fence. There was a chicken coop back there along the back of the property. There was a screened-in porch along the back of the house where Granny had her church meetings and did her sewing. She was always sewing, either that or canning. And the church ladies were there almost every day, praying and singing and praising God with their Hallelujahs.

When she was sewing, Granny would be making her ankle-length drab-colored dresses or making me shirts from flours sacks. She and her friends would chip in to buy the flour, then they'd divide it up among them. When that was done Granny would bleach out the sacks to remove the label that was printed on them. Then she'd die them blue or green and cut them into patterns to make shirts or shorts for me. Then she'd sew the buttons and zippers on them and they were ready to wear.

The house had three bedrooms and a bathroom on one side with a long hall running down it. On the other side of the house going from front to back were a living room, a dining room and the kitchen. The living room had a couch, three chairs and a radio in it; behind it was the dining room with a simple walnut table and six chairs; and behind that room were the kitchen and pantry.

The back yard of that house was gigantic—at least it was to me. There was the big walnut tree with a huge knothole in it way out by the back fence. There was also the chicken coop out by the back fence where Grandpa raised a brood of chickens that gave us eggs. That chicken shack would later serve as a source of education for me, but we'll get to that a little later on.

What I mostly remember about that neighborhood—from what little I could see of it, restricted as I was by Granny to a two-block radius around our house—were the number of trains that ran nearby.

There were freight trains and streetcars and the Big Red Line of the Pacific Electric Company that were all within blocks of us. The #5 streetcar line was the longest one in Los Angeles, running from Hawthorne way out to the southwest to Pasadena way out in the northeast. There was one other thing in our neighborhood that captured my attention and that was the big Goodyear Tire Company plant that was just to the west of us on the other side of Gage Street.

In the field near the plant sat the Goodyear blimp. For one day at least that plant would prove to be the most eye-opening experience for me during those hard years of the Depression with Grandma and Grandpa.

The Great Depression hit Los Angeles very hard, and though most people know it today as a big event in American history, most people have no personal recollection of it.

Sometimes I wish I didn't.

What I remember most about that hard time was that everybody was always looking for something to eat and that nobody seemed to have any money. When you walked down the street people would be standing there asking "Can you help? Can you help?" and holding out their hands. Most people in Florence couldn't. Everybody was almost as dirt poor as the folks out begging were. Granny did her Christian do-gooder best to help the poor by making patchwork quilts for them on her sewing machine with her Bible-thumping friends. But almost everybody I saw in Los Angeles during those years was scratching and scrounging just to stay alive.

That's what all those vegetable gardens were about in our section of town. They were an absolute necessity to have if you wanted to stay alive. Granny grew carrots, cabbage, turnips and beans out there. But her specialty was tomatoes, which was a prime source of nourishment for her and Grandpa and me.

She'd pick the tomatoes when they were ripe and

bring them in and put them in a big kettle to stew them over the gas stove. When they were done, she'd slice them into thirds and put one slice each on a piece of bread, then she'd sprinkle sugar on top and put another piece of bread on top of it all. She'd serve one each to me, Grandpa, and herself.

She served those stewed tomatoes sandwiches to us at least five times a week. I got to the point where I couldn't stand them, and just the smell of the stewing tomatoes could almost make me throw up. To this day I can't eat a tomato unless it's fresh; the smell of cooking tomatoes brings those hard Depression times right back home to me. But I ate *every* stewed tomato sandwich that was put in front of me back then. What choice did I have? It was stewed tomato sandwiches or starve.

I did what I could back then to help my family survive during those hard days. Although I usually wasn't allowed to associate with other kids in the neighborhood I did have one friend who lived at the end of the block that I could see. His name was Johnny and he lived nearby the railroad tracks. He and I and my dog Mickey would go out and wait for a freight train to pass. When one did, we'd chase after it and beg for coal pieces from the conductor, who'd usually throw us a chunk or two. From those handouts and the few odd pieces that we found lying along the track, Johnny and I were able to contribute to our households and keep our families warm during the cold winter nights when we'd burn the coal in our coal-fired stoves.

It was also over at Johnny's house where I learned a little bit about mature human anatomy. One day I walked down there and saw his dad working on his truck. He had the hood up and was working with a monkey wrench. But when he came out from under the hood and started working on some other part of the truck, I saw that his overalls had been ripped in the crotch. I saw this massive, hairy thing dangling there. I thought, *Oh, my God, what the hell is that thing? Is this what's going to happen to me when I grow up?* When Johnny's old man turned around, he saw the look on my face and quickly realized the source of it. He scooted back inside the house and changed into a different pair of overalls while Johnny and I howled with laughter.

Our daily life back in those Depression days was pretty simple. In the mornings Grandma would wake me up and then she and Grandpa and I would sit down to a simple breakfast of Cream of Wheat or oatmeal. Every so often we'd have a plate of bacon and eggs or ham and eggs. Afterwards I'd walk to school alone, sometimes meeting a kid or two along the way.

It was a school called the Florence Normal School, grades one through nine, and it was located about half a mile west of our home on 69th and Converse. A bus or a streetcar line would take you directly to the school, but we had so little money then that I usually walked. There would sometimes be plays held at school and there were theaters in our neighborhood, including the Million Dollar Fox Theater, just down on Florence Boulevard.

But Grandma discouraged such extracurricular activities. They conflicted with her religious beliefs as a Nazarene Christian and I wasn't allowed to attend any plays or movies or do the other things that other kids did back then. The only people I was allowed to associate with back then were my grandparents and their adult friends. And every now and then I'd be allowed to go off with Johnny on one of our coal-collecting expeditions.

Most of the adults I knew in those days were Grandma's friends from church, and I saw the inside of more churches than I care to remember.

There was Granny's Nazarene Christian Church, an old brick building at the corner of Florence and Vermont Streets. We'd also got to Baptist churches, Methodist churches, and Episcopal churches. You name it. Everything but synagogues and Catholic churches were fair game. And we didn't just go on Sundays; sometimes we'd go three or four times a week, more if Grandma thought it was necessary. Like I said, for her it was a daily deal, every day.

Once a month we'd travel into downtown Los Angeles on a streetcar and attend the Angelus Temple on Glendale near Sunset. It had just opened back then and was run by Aimee Semple McPherson, a longhaired blonde babe who dressed in long pearly white robes. She was a celebrity back then, despite a scandal that she'd gotten involved in sometime in the 1920s right before I was born. It had something to do with her strange disappearance. They finally discovered her in some No-Tell Motel with a man. They all hushed it up and she was on outs with the church for a while. But by the 1930s the church had forgiven her and she had repented, I guess. Aimee thanked the church by building this big fancy temple for them.

Almost all of these churches had Bible study classes and other programs for children. But I was never allowed to attend any of them. Granny wanted to keep me right with her where she sat with all her adult Bible-thumper girlfriends. We sang hymns and prayed until we were hoarse. That whole thing sort of distorted me, and I could tell that even back then. Adults defined my whole world. It was defined by their behavior—by what they said and thought. It was really my only point of reference for the entire time that I lived with Grandma and Grandpa.

Church and school, school and church—and sometimes foraging for scraps of coal with Johnny and Mickey my dog. That's what I remember the most of those poor, grim days in Florence, California. Granny picking her tomatoes and stewing them until the smell of it made me sick. There just wasn't much variation then—in either my life or my diet. The only other supplements to our daily fare came from the merchants who came to our house to deliver their goods.

The iceman would come in a big truck to deliver the ice that provided the refrigeration for keeping our food fresh. Every other day, the milkman would come and deliver a couple of quarts of milk with the delicious heavy cream on top. They were mostly Dutchmen from down in Maywood, a little town southwest of us between Inglewood and Long Beach, out near where I later lived with The Redhead. Once a week the vegetable man would come with fresh vegetables, carrying them in a horse-drawn wagon. Then on Fridays the fish man would come out in a refrigerated truck carrying fresh fish that he brought in from Wilmington, Long Beach and San Pedro, where the fishing boats pulled in and unloaded. Those folks were the only intruders who interrupted our daily routine back then in Florence.

Still, despite the monotony of the routine that hardly changed from day to day and the poverty that we all had to endure back then, there were occasional glimpses into a wider world that was fascinating to me. And sometimes those glimpses into this unknown world were amazing. One of those things was the world of the gypsies.

They'd come to town once a year—a whole band of them, maybe a hundred or so, in colorful trucks and buses and automobiles that were just this side of totally broken down. I'd never seen people like them before, and to a child such as I was back then, anything that was as out of the ordinary as the gypsies were was an eye-opening experience.

They were dark and swarthy. The men dressed in strange-looking shirts with bolero sleeves and wore strange colored shiny pants that were also kind of ballooned. They had thick black hair and big mustaches and spoke a different language in a sort of growl. The women wore colorful printed dresses and turbans that covered their heads and didn't say much. The kids that came with them were equally strange-looking whenever you could see them. But the gypsy adults mostly kept them out of sight except when they took them out in the street with them to go begging.

Grandma and Grandpa and most of the other adults in Florence or from the church were scared to death of the gypsies. The only time we were allowed to get near them was when they'd put on their big show down by the railroad tracks to the southeast of us where they had their camp.

The men would come out and do sword swallowing, knife throwing and fire breathing. The women would come out and sing and dance and twirl around banging tambourines and other noisemaking things. But as far as the adults in my grandparents' circle were concerned, that was as much as they could take of the gypsies. They said the gypsies were notorious for thievery and said they ran con games with fortune telling. Once when I said something to Grandma about them, asking if I could go over to their camp with Johnny so we could watch them, she said "Absolutely not. They might kidnap you and have you for dinner."

So ended my childhood fascination with the exotic world of the gypsies.

Not long after my gypsy period, the Martians invaded.

It was five o'clock on October 30, 1938, when the Martians invaded. Grandpa and I were listening to the radio when Orson Welles came on to announce that a big burning object had landed on a farm in New Jersey. We sat there staring at one another while Welles kept rattling on with news of the Martian invasion. They were big as bears with skin like leather and big gleaming eyes. They were armed with death rays and the New Jersey militia was fighting them. Total pandemonium was about to break out.

Grandma joined us and we kept listening to the frightening reports. There were Martian sightings in other states and everybody was absolutely terrified. After a while we went outside and looked into the night sky above Los Angeles to see if there were Martians invading us, too. By the time that we got outside most of our neighbors were out there too looking into the night sky. There were shouts of "There's one of their spaceships twinkling over there."

But it was all a big hoax put on by Orson Welles, and it was all over the news the next day.

So the Martians were a no-show. The gypsies were a forbidden show, and maybe cooked non-gypsy kids and ate them for dinner. Movies were off limits, so were school plays and team sports. But once every year, the one show that I was allowed to go to would come to town and it was the "Greatest Show On Earth." It was when the Ringling Brothers Circus pulled into L.A.

On the day of the circus they'd let all of us kids out of school for the day. The teachers and some of the kids' moms or dads would haul us into downtown Los Angeles in their cars—five or six kids in each—and we'd go in to watch the circus unload at the Southern-Pacific freight station. The circus handlers would put ramps up to the freight cars where the animals were housed. Then they'd open the doors and march the animals down the ramps. Elephants and horses, tigers and lions, giraffes and zebras—you name it, the Ringling Brothers had 'em. They'd put the dangerous ones like the lions and tigers in cages and load them into trucks with bars on the sides so you could still see them through it. But the elephants and horses and the zebras and giraffes and the circus performers themselves walked right down the street from the S-P yards to the circus tents in the vacant lot about ten or fifteen blocks away. We kids would form into the "Greatest Show on Earth." Then all of us the audience would stand and cheer and clap like mad. And the fun would begin.

The tigers would jump through flaming hoops. The lions would do their thing and roar. The strong man would come out dressed in a sort of Tarzan outfit and lift giant barbells above his head. The sword-swallowers and flame-breathers would perform their routines and they were even better than the gypsies were. Then the pretty girls would come out and stand on the horses' and zebras' backs and ride them around. Then one of them would stand against a turning wheel and have knives thrown at her, which used to scare the hell out of us kids. We wondered how the knife thrower could get so close to her and not hit her and how he could aim with a wheel turning in back of her.

From the unloading of the animals in the freight yards until the final act, we saw the whole show. And by the time that we were transported back to school and then walked home from there, it was already time for supper, then off to bed quickly after that. The next day, it was back to the usual daily grind.

The other amusements that were available to me in Los Angeles back then were few and far between. The Depression had hit Los Angeles hard and it had put an end to the city's great expansion of the 1920s. That expansion was fueled by oil discovery and suburban growth. In the decade of the 1920s, the city's population swelled from 600,000 to 1,200,000. New towns were being built all over the L.A. basin. Hollywood was then in its heyday, and the motion picture studios were doing major business. Then the Depression hit.

The new towns that were scattering from Los Angeles to Long Beach and from L.A. through the San Fernando Valley stopped scattering in the 1930s. The golden suburban growth period had all panned out.

Since Grandma's strict religiousness and her regular strict nature prohibiting me from having regular kid fun were enforced with an iron fist, there wasn't much I could do. Nor was there anybody I was allowed to do much with, except Grandpa.

Maybe he took pity on me. Maybe it was because he wasn't cut from the same severe religious cloth that Grandma was. But pretty soon Grandpa and I became good pals and we began doing things together that didn't include Grandma.

Sometimes Grandpa would take me with him on his various odd jobs where I'd help him doing carpentry or janitorial chores. But that wasn't too often. Where we spent most of our time together was out in that big back yard that looked out on the Goodyear plant.

There was that huge walnut tree back there, maybe eighty feet high with branches that spread over a thirty-foot diameter. There was a big Y in the tree just about six feet up it and there was a huge knothole there where the main upper branches forked. In that fork Grandpa would stick an old piece of mirror. Then he'd pull out a giant steel file and start filing away on his teeth. He did it to take off the tobacco stains that came from chewing tobacco, and I guess it worked. But, God, I'll never forget the sound that the file made as he stood there looking in the mirror and grinding away at his teeth. Finally, when that routine was over, I'd go out to the chicken coop with him and help him feed the chickens.

Then, when I got a little older—somewhere around seven or eight, I think—Grandpa introduced me to beer.

I don't recall the exact circumstances of how the beer thing came around, but one day Grandpa fished in his overall pocket and pulled out a dime. He sent me down an alley to a nearby store and told me to use a certain knock followed by two short whistles. "Now when that door opens, Russ, the man, will hand you a pail filled with something. Then you give him the dime and he'll give you some change. Then you hurry back here as fast as you can. And one other thing, Claude; don't spill what's in that pail."

Grandma must have been out with her church friends. Maybe Grandpa had sent her off on some other errand, or else he never would have risked it. I ran all the way down the alley to the store, did the secret knocks and two short whistles, and the man put a pail in my hand. I gave him the dime and he gave me a nickel change. The bucket was full to the brim and I hurried back home, trying not to slop any of it out on the ground. Then when I got there Grandpa poured himself a glass from the bucket. He drained it and poured himself another. Then he pulled out a smaller glass, filled it, and handed it to me. I sipped it at first then did what Grandpa did with his. I drained it.

My God, it was delicious! For me, it was a true religious experience. And though I am not a beer drinker today, whenever it happens to be a very hot day in Florence, Oregon, which is very rare, I think about those beer-drinking sessions in the chicken coop with Grandpa.

We drank and talked, talked and drank some more until we'd emptied the pail, sitting in the back of that chicken coop with the hens and rooster pecking about. We'd sit all the way back in the corner of the coop so if Grandma happened to come out she wouldn't be able to see us and what we were doing. Now as I tried to recall those conversations, I draw a blank. Maybe it's the Alzheimer's, but what does it matter anyway? It was just a guy thing—comradeship, I guess. We certainly didn't talk about sports, because I didn't play team sports and didn't know anything about them.

I think that maybe Grandpa sensed that the kind of life I was leading wasn't much of a kid's life at all; that it was too full of churches and adults and there wasn't much relief from it. I think maybe that's why he introduced me to beer. I do know that Grandpa wasn't the religious red hot that Grandma was and I think he grew bored with all the church ladies and their yammering about the Lord and all. Sometimes he'd make up excuses to leave the house when they came around. Sometimes he'd make an excuse for me and take me with him. Maybe he sensed that my religiousness was more like his, because I was none too fond of all that Holy Roller shit that Grandma and her friends tossed around.

Grandpa almost had a sixth sense of when I'd reached my limit with the daily routine of God, adults and scrounging. He must have read it in my eyes or my body posture or something. Because when I did get to that point, he'd send Grandma off on some errand or wait until she was occupied with some chore and then he'd reach in his pocket and fish out a dime and tell me that he needed me to run a special errand for him.

He'd give me a wink and tell me that he'd meet me back in the chicken coop. My eyes would light up and I'd fly out of that house and sprint down the alley. Then I'd give the special knock, do the double whistle, and then do my balancing act with the beer on my way back. When I did get back there Grandpa would be looking in that little mirror set on the knothole, filing the tobacco stains off of his teeth.

As far as weekend excursions went, there just weren't many of them. Other than the once a month pilgrimage that Granny and I would make to Aimee's Angelus Temple out on Glendale Boulevard, we stayed pretty close to home. Sometimes if it was nice outside and Grandpa happened to catch Grandma in the right mood, we might go to one of the parks that were fairly close to us.

There was Elysian Park, just a few miles north of us where there were trails through the arroyo along the banks f the Los Angeles River, and where there were picnic grounds and free water and free firewood so families could have a picnic. And there was Exposition park, up by USC, with the History and Science Museum that we'd sometimes go to.

But those trips were rare—maybe once a month—and most weekends were spent with Grandpa and Grandma and I and their adult friends at our house on Converse, sitting and talking and listening to the radio.

Sometimes during that period in the late 1930s—a summer night is all I remember—Grandpa and I were sitting out back in the chicken coop drinking beer when a huge commotion came up just to the west of our house. When I looked over that way I saw a bright lighted area and asked Grandpa what it was. "There's a prize fight going on," he said. I could hear an announcer's voice and a cheering crowd. Then the fight started.

We could hear the boxers' gloves as they made contact with each other. It didn't go on for long. We could hear the solid punches of the winning boxer slamming into the loser's skull, hitting him so hard that he started screaming. Then the crowd noise changed and went from cheering to yelling for the referee to stop it. I guess he did, because the crowd noise died out to a murmur and then the lights went out. Grandpa and I sat there drinking our beer. Then finally Grandpa said something. "Armstrong wins again," he said. Then he asked me if I thought I'd like to see a prize fight, and I wagged my head no. "I don't think so, Grandpa," I said. "I'd rather just drink beer with you out here in the chicken coop." He laughed, toasted me, and we drained our glasses dry.

Almost every day of my youth I used to look across the street and see the Goodyear blimp sitting there out in the field. There was a neighbor couple that lived on the Goodyear property and the man had a job working in the Goodyear plant as well as being the property watchman. Over time, he and Grandpa and I became friendly and he'd sometimes come over and talk to us when we'd go out to the coop.

One day, the man whose name I've long forgotten, came over and asked me if I'd like to visit the plant with him one day. Actually he asked Grandpa if it would be OK. Grandpa said that he'd consider it but he'd first have to clear it with his wife.

That night, he started working on Grandma.

The negotiations dragged on for weeks. About every

other night after dinner Grandpa would send me off to the front room to listen to the radio while he worked on Grandma on the back porch. "Come on, Ella," he'd say, "what's the harm in the kid going over to see the plant? Let him go see the blimp." Grandma was mostly silent. She said that she didn't know the couple, that maybe they were heathens who'd have a bad influence on me. Back and forth, it went. Then, one day after breakfast, Grandpa got up from the table and motioned for me to follow him. "Come on, youngster," he said. "Let's go see our neighbor and see if his offer's still good."

We went over to the house and Grandpa got the neighbor's attention. The man came over to the fence and he and Grandpa wandered off a few paces and talked. The arrangements were made, and I was to come to work with the neighbor man about a week later, a Monday I remember. Then Grandma went to school with me and told them that I'd be taking that day off to visit the Goodyear plant. The school agreed. It was all set.

On the day of my visit, Grandpa took me over to the neighbor's house and told the man to have me home by suppertime. Then he returned to me and said: "Go on, Claude. Go with the man and see the blimp. Then when you get home you can tell Grandma and me all about it."

It was to be the greatest day of my young life. It was magic. Pure magic. We toured the plant and the neighbor showed me the process that Goodyear used to build tires. The warehouses that they did it in were huge and the machines that they used to make the tires were gigantic and strange and made strange noises when they were operating. We walked all the way through the tire-making process—from the vats of molten rubber all the way to the finishing touches when they were stamped with the

Goodyear mark. Then it was time for the ride in the blimp.

We climbed up a short set of wooden stairs and got into the little cockpit of the blimp that was on the bottom of it. There was a pilot inside with a radio headset on and there were a bunch of controls and gauges in front of him and he explained them all to me. Then he got on the radio and talked to the tower and after a minute or so they cleared us for takeoff.

We seemed to go almost straight up, rising above the plant, and when I looked down I could see Grandpa and Grandma waving to me from the backyard. Then we headed west and flew out towards the coast and the pilot and the neighbor man pointed out all the landmarks for me. There was Long Beach where my uncle and aunt and cousins lived, and there was Santa Monica and the pier with the amusement park on it. Then we turned north, heading up the coast, and in the distance I could see Santa Catalina Island. The whole world was visible from here in the blimp it seemed to me. We turned east and cruised over Westwood, where UCLA was, then Hollywood and Eagle Rock, then Pasadena, Glendale and the San Gabriel Mountains. There was Arroyo Seco and downtown Los Angeles, then finally back home again where we seemed to drop straight back down to our starting point with the little flight of stairs. Then it was over. But it didn't leave me, ever.

When the neighbor couple took me back to my house, Grandma and Grandpa were waiting for me, and all of us, the neighbors included, had a great supper of chicken and dumplings that evening while I told Grandma and Grandpa all about the plant and the blimp. I filled their ears with every detail I could remember of what I saw and did and how it felt until I was finally sent to bed.

The next day when I went to school my teacher asked me to share my experience at the Goodyear plant with the whole class. She made me get up in front of them to tell them all about it. So I did. I told them all about the plant and how tires were made with all the different machines and I told them of my ride in the blimp and all that I saw from up there in the clouds. And for that one day and most of the rest of the week I was pretty much the class hero, I guess. Everybody wanted to be my friend and hear the tale again and again. It made me feel good, almost like all the suffering and strictness and scraping to get by had been worth something. It took me out of my small, enclosed, restricted world and showed me a wider one where anything seemed possible.

As I grew older—around age eight or so—I began to get the feeling that the life I lived at home was far different from the ones that my fellow classmates lived. The people in my home were older than the people in their homes. The other kids had mothers and fathers they lived with, not grandparents, although they had them, too. But up until that time I had never seen my parents, only heard about them, and that wasn't too often.

The only time that I heard about my father, whose name was Claude like mine is, was when I was five years old. I got up on the morning of my fifth birthday and there in the living room was a brand new bike. "Your father brought that for your birthday, Claude," my Grandma told me. I had never had a bike before, much less ridden one very much. I tried it out a few times with Grandpa coaching me how to operate it and was just starting to get the hang of it. Then one day when I came home from school I found my bike sitting all mangled up in the front yard. A neighbor had backed his car over it, Grandma said. Grandpa and I tried to do what we could to fix it, but it was entirely wrecked. I never heard from my father again.

Still, I now knew that I had a father, and that he couldn't have been such a bad guy having bought me a brand new bike and all. But as for my mother it was a different story. I never heard from her, and what I heard about her wasn't too good.

Grandma and Grandpa would never talk about her in front of me. They'd wait until I was in the living room or in my bedroom and I'd have to listen in on their private conversations about her. They'd say things like "Well, I heard from The Redhead today. She's on her way up to San Francisco." Or they'd say, "I ran into so-and-so and he said he ran into The Redhead the other day."

It seemed as though neither Grandma or Grandpa thought very highly of her, and Grandma used to shake her head sometimes and say "I can't believe that something like that came out of me. How did she turn out so bad coming out of a good Christian woman like me?" Grandpa would do what he could for her to calm her down, but it sometimes didn't work. Grandma would break down and cry. Then she'd go off to her room and pray or lie down for a while.

I was still too young then to understand what all the commotion about The Redhead was about and why she had such a bad effect on my Grandma. It confused me when they talked about her. They said that she was bad, that she was a tramp.

I would soon learn for myself what all the commotion and tears were about. I was about to meet The Redhead, and that would prove to be an experience that I still haven't gotten over, not even to this day.

Three
The Redhead

It was a hot day in June, the last day of school, June 10, 1938, and I was walking home with some friends of mine. They'd let us out early that day, and I'd just completed the third grade. I was nine years old. We were walking eastward on 69th, just past Compton Avenue near the fire station and within blocks of Grandpa's and Grandma's house, when my friends and I parted company. We said our goodbyes in front of a vacant lot. Then all hell broke loose. The Redhead arrived and my life was about to change.

I had walked only a few steps by myself when a bottle-green Model A Ford screeched to a halt beside me. The passenger's side window opened and I saw a woman with really long red hair who was driving the car. There was a bullet hole in the front windshield on the driver's side. "Get in," she said. "I'm your mother and you're coming with me." I was alarmed by what she said and couldn't think clearly about what I should do. I had only heard about her—my mother—and what I'd heard about her was none too good.

I knew that my mother had red hair. So did this woman in the green Model A. Finally I did what she said and got in the car.

I was about to find out for myself what Grandma and

Grandpa knew. She was trouble, big trouble, nothing but trouble. And though I'd been through hard times with Grandma and Grandpa, they couldn't hold a candle to the living, scorching ride to hell and back that I was about to go through with The Redhead.

I opened the car door. The Redhead grabbed my wrist and yanked me into the car. "Get down," she said, pushing me down on the floorboards. Then she hung a U turn, and headed west, driving fast.

Eventually she told me to get up off the floorboards and sit on the seat next to her. I did as she said but kept my distance from her.

I looked at her as we drove west. She was small and pretty, that much I could tell. She was wearing perfume and lipstick—something that Grandma never did—and she was chain-smoking cigarettes.

We drove for miles and miles, heading west on Florence Boulevard, until we got to Inglewood. Then we stopped in front of a store and she made me get out with her and go in. It was a second-hand store with furniture and clothes and tools in it. "I want to buy this kid some clothes," she told the saleslady. The woman she said it to came over and asked me to follow her. She picked out three shirts and two pairs of pants that fit me. Then she had me try on some shoes until we found a pair that fit. Then The Redhead paid the lady and told me to pick up the bag and follow her back to the car.

Finally I asked a question. "How did this car get a bullet hole in it?" I said. She said that someone had taken a shot at her. She said it happened when she was working undercover for the cops. Then she told me to shut up and mind my own business and off we went.

We drove to a house in what was then called Lennox. It was a little town then, right on the eastern edge of what is now the Los Angeles International Airport. The house was a little brown stucco bungalow, and it was much smaller than Grandpa and Grandma's house on Converse. There were only two bedrooms in it, not three. We pulled the car into the driveway, drove back towards the garage, and then stopped. The Redhead got out of the car and opened my door and told me to follow her. I grabbed my bag of new old clothes and did what she said. She opened the side door of the garage and guided me inside. "You wait right here. Don't move and don't say a word and I'll be right back," she said. I stood there in the dark. I was scared out of my wits and growing numb with fear.

A minute later, she returned. She had some blankets and a little throw pillow under her arm. She made up a bed for me in the corner of the garage and told me to sit on it and be quiet until she came back. I heard the Model A start up, then heard it back out of the driveway. About an hour later The Redhead returned with a sandwich and a bottle of milk. "Here, this is your supper," she said. "Now don't you dare make a sound if you know what's good for you."

I didn't. I was too scared to do anything. I ate my supper then sat down on the bed and cried as quietly as I could. Eventually I fell asleep.

That's how my days with The Redhead began. I would only be with her for a year and a half at first, then for a few months after that. But all of it was a torturous time of physical and emotional and psychological abuse that has taken me almost a lifetime to get over.

No, that's not entirely correct. In some ways I still haven't gotten over it, and I still haven't figured out what motivated The Redhead to treat me the way that she did.

She went by the name of Peggy, and signed all her

notes and letters with that name. She wrote a lot of notes and letters and had pen pals all over the United States. But her real name was Ila Ona Baker. She was born on November 10, 1909 in Galveston, Texas. Her father's name was Milt Baker. Her mother's name was Ella, my grandmother.

Ella and Milt were originally from Topeka, Kansas, where they were married in 1908. The Redhead also had a sister named Jewell, who was a couple of years younger than she. Her father moved the family down to Texas where he had a job working in the oil fields. He died there in an accident one day while he was working on an oil rig. My Grandma Ella buried him back in Kansas then took her two girls with her and went to Los Angeles where she had relatives. I have no clue as to what The Redhead's younger years in Los Angeles were like, but I can imagine she grew up fast.

When she was nineteen she married my father. His name was Claude Russell, and he had a twin brother named Clint. The Redhead had dated Clint for awhile before she married my father. By the time she swooped in and scooped me off the sidewalk into the green Model A, she'd been married two more times since leaving my father.

. . . Meanwhile, back in the garage. The next morning after she stuck me out there she came out early with two pieces of toast with jam on them and a glass of milk. "Breakfast," she said. "Get up and get dressed. We're leaving here in twenty minutes." I did as I was told, slipping on the used clothes she'd bought the day before putting the rest of it in a sack.

When she returned a few minutes later she was all dolled up in a tight print dress, wearing lipstick and other makeup and smelling of perfume. She packed me into the

Model A, fired up one of her Domino cigarettes, backed up into the street and zoomed off towards Los Angeles.

I was still too scared to talk much but since we were heading back east I thought she was taking me back to Grandpa's and Grandma's. Then we passed through the Florence section and didn't stop. I was wrong.

We headed north on the Arroyo Seco freeway, the first freeway built in Los Angeles. We drove north, heading towards Pasadena. "Aren't we going to Grandpa and Grandma's?" I finally asked. The Redhead shot me a glare with those cold green eyes and took a drag on her cigarette. "You forget about Grandma and Grandpa for a while. Let me worry about that. I'm your mother and you're coming with me."

I shut up and looked out the window, watching the suburbs go by. We passed through Eagle Rock, then Highland Park, then Pasadena, still heading east until we were in the high desert. The Redhead didn't say a word and didn't stop driving until we were way out of town.

We finally got to Riverside, about sixty miles east of Los Angeles. She pulled up to a gas station, stopped the car, and had the attendant fill the tank. I could see her asking the attendant something, giving him a big smile and showing off her bright white teeth. He wrote something down on a piece of paper and handed it to her.

When she got back in the car, she followed the directions that the attendant had written on the paper. Eventually we pulled up in front of a big fenced compound with a sign on the outside. The Riverside Reformatory was what the sign read. She pulled through the gate and parked the car in front and told me to get out and bring my things and follow her. She marched me in front of her to the administration building. We walked inside then went down a long hall to an office where a man sat behind a desk.

"You must be Mrs. Messler," he said.

She said that she was. Now The Redhead had a name, Mrs. Messler.

"Then this must be your son, Claude?"

"That's him," she said, pointing at me.

"Well, Mrs. Messler. Just exactly what did Claude do that makes you think that The Riverside Reformatory would be good for him?"

The Redhead told him a huge pack of lies. She said that I lied and stole, that I was a problem in school and bothered other school kids. She said I never told the truth, that I cheated at games and was just bad all the way around. All of this was coming from a woman who I'd never even seen until the day before, and who had no way of knowing what I did in school or how I was with other children. All of this was coming from the woman who claimed to be my mother, a woman who had never mothered me so far as I knew. I sat there stunned, listening to her rattle off these lies.

"But really, Mrs. Messler, just how bad is he? Is he really that bad a boy?" As he said this, the administrator kept looking me over.

"Oh, he's pretty bad all right—really bad. My husband and I can't do a thing with him," The Redhead said.

The man told her that the reform school would take me in. He handed her some papers and she signed them. Then somebody came in and told me to follow him and he'd show me back to my dorm. As I was leaving the room The Redhead called out one last parting shot to me. "Maybe this'll toughen you up, kid," she said.

That concluded my first encounter with The Redhead. Later I realized that my mother hadn't even touched me, much less kissed me or hugged me. I wouldn't see her again for another three months.

I then began my life in reform school. It was a place filled with petty criminals, juvenile hard cases and misfits. Now I was one of them. We ranged in age from eight to seventeen.

How did I wind up here? I'd ask myself. I'd never once been in trouble up until then. I attended school every day that I was supposed to, except for that one heroic day on the blimp. I wasn't a genius at school, but I was smart enough to earn B's and C's with an occasional A. I didn't do bad things like cheat or lie. That was sort of impossible given the kind of Holy Roller environment that Grandma insisted I maintain back at our house in Florence. My only crime up to that time was the beer drinking that I used to do with Grandpa back in the chicken coop. Now I was an inmate in a reform school, and for how long I had no way of knowing.

The routine at The Riverside Reformatory was Spartan and military. A loud bell would ring out in the morning, and it meant that we had fifteen minutes to go to the bathroom, brush our teeth, make our beds and stand for attention and morning count. When that was done, we marched down the hall in single file and went to the cafeteria for a breakfast that was barely edible. We'd get oatmeal or runny eggs and undercooked potatoes, grits and toast, things like that.

At quarter to seven another bell would ring and then all of us reform school inmates would scramble outside onto an asphalt lot out back where we'd exercise for thirty minutes. We did push ups, jumping jacks, toe touches, and then run a few laps around the asphalt lot. Then we were hustled back inside where we had thirty minutes to shower and get dressed. At eight o'clock another bell rang and we'd march off for class. We'd stand for another inspection beside our desks. If you passed, nothing happened. If you didn't—if your shirt wasn't tucked in right, or your hair wasn't parted right, or your shoes weren't shined properly—then you'd get a beating. Right there in front of the other kids the instructor would pull out a short whip and let you have it. You'd get anywhere from three to ten lashes with it, sometimes until you bled.

School didn't last long during those hot summer days—maybe two hours was all we had. What we mostly did with our day was work. Usually it was in the open fields nearby where there were watermelon and cantaloupe patches. We'd pick the ripe fruit and then stack it in the spots where they were picked up later by trucks. We worked with our hands and backs, bent over under the broiling summer sun. We worked with picks and shovels, moving dirt or manure around. We'd work until 4:30, sometimes later when there was some deadline that had to be met or if they just felt like working us harder. We did what we were told to do.

I was a small kid then—not even five feet tall and maybe sixty-five pounds dripping wet. Because I was a newcomer and didn't know anybody well, I was usually given the shit detail. The older kids in the reformatory would often force younger kids like me to do their jobs for them. They'd do this as soon as the guards left the work area and found some shady spot to rest in. You did what the older kids told you to do. You took one helluva beating from them if you didn't.

If this is what The Redhead meant by toughening me up, she sure wasn't joking. During the course of that long hot summer of 1938 I began to develop muscles and upper body strength. But I sure didn't like it.

I did the best that I could while I was in The Riverside Reformatory to avoid any trouble. I followed the rules, did the jobs that were assigned me, and some of the other ones that the older, bigger kids told me to do that they were assigned and didn't want to do. I avoided fights, but there were plenty of them that I saw during that summer. Usually they were between the older kids, and as I said some of them were already hardened criminals by then. Finally, in early September, The Redhead came back out to Riverside to fetch me back to her house in Lennox.

That didn't mean that there was going to be any relief from her tortures. Now she had a new place to stick me in. And while it didn't involve the kind of physical torture that the reform school did, it involved a particular sort of mental and psychological terror that nothing in my life had yet prepared me for. What The Redhead did was stick me in a Catholic school.

First we drove back to the little stucco bungalow in Lennox. This time I didn't have to sleep in the garage. She took me into the house where a bedroom had been set up for me. It was just a little room with a bed and an end table next to it with a lamp on it. There was also a battered wooden dresser with four drawers, giving me a place to put my things, such as they were. All of the furniture came from that same second-hand store over in Inglewood that we'd stopped at some months back.

The Redhead came in and told me where to put my things and I followed her orders. Then that evening when he got home from work, I met her new husband. He was a guy named Hank Messler.

Hank seemed like a nice guy. He was a hard-working man who owned a little deli down in Hawthorne, the next town south of us. He was quiet and kind and laid back, and over the next few days before school started that fall, Hank befriended me.

At least Hank talked to me, and that was something The Redhead just didn't do. All that she did was bark orders and curses at me. She'd tell me what she needed and wanted from me as she sat there in the front room lounging on the sofa, listening to the radio and chain-smoking her Domino cigarettes. Sometimes she'd send me down to the store to fetch a new pack when she was running low. She'd give me a dime and send me off, and I'd have to bring the three cents in change back to her.

On the Sunday before the fall semester was set to begin, Hank took me out for a whole day with him. We got in his car and headed out early. The Redhead didn't come with us. Where she was, I didn't know. Nor did I care, given what I'd seen from her so far. Hank and I drove down to Hermosa Beach, where we fished from the pier and then ate lunch at a diner. Then we headed back home and Hank fixed a nice dinner for me and him. The Redhead still hadn't gotten home by then.

The next morning she was back. She came in and woke me up early, told me to get cleaned and dressed, then served me some oatmeal and took me to my new school. It was a few miles east of us down Florence Boulevard, back in Los Angeles proper. It was a Catholic school called St. Mary's Academy. Looking back on it now, there didn't seem too much that was holy about that place, and they sure didn't seem to have much more kindness than the folks at the reformatory did.

It was almost a repeat of that first scene three months before at the reformatory. She packed me into the bullet-holed Model A. We drove to the administration building, and were directed down the hall to the principal's office. He was a man named Monsignor So-and-so.

He was wearing a long black robe and a stiff white cardboard collar that matched his white hair.

The Redhead told the monsignor about what a bad boy I was. She said that I was a thief, a liar and a cheat. She told him I didn't get along with other kids my age. She told him that I didn't pay attention. The monsignor sat there, nodding along to her lies as she filled his ear with all this bullshit that I never did and that she'd never seen or even had the opportunity to see. I sat there listening to this made-up yarn that she had concocted, but I was still too scared of her to raise my voice and say anything about it. That was something that kids from the Depression just didn't do. Adults ruled the world, and whatever they said was accepted as true. Kids back then did what they were told, didn't talk back, and generally kept quiet.

Finally the monsignor said something. He leaned back, looked at me hard and told The Redhead "Well, Mrs. Messler, I think you've brought Claude to the right place. We'll straighten him out and make a good Catholic boy out of him."

"Do whatever you have to do," said The Redhead. "My husband and I have done the best we could and we'd appreciate a hand. Maybe you can help us. Sure, make a good Catholic boy out of him," she said.

The Redhead got up, smoothed her dress and shook the monsignor's hand. Then he pulled out some papers and had her sign them. He looked at me coldly, said good-bye to The Redhead, and told me to follow him.

We marched down the hall to a classroom where there were maybe sixty kids inside and one adult. It was the teacher, and it seemed she was a woman, but she was unlike any woman I'd ever seen before. She wore a long black robe like the monsignor did, but hers was more of a dress than a robe like his was. She had some strange headdress on, too. It was a long black veil thing, with a white sort of crown on top. She was called Sister Something or Other. I was about to learn about nuns and I was about to find out why Grandma didn't particularly like Catholics.

I only had to go to the Saint Mary's Academy for a semester, and I was certainly glad of that. The nuns weren't quite as brutal as The Redhead was, but like her they seemed to take a certain kind of glee from the cruelty that they handed out to children.

They preached at us and called us sinners who were on our way to Hell. If we weren't headed there, we were headed to a place called Purgatory. Both of these places were on fire with flames that would never die. The only difference between the two was that Hell was permanent while Purgatory was only temporary. Both of these places were below the earth and everybody who was sentenced there was constantly screaming in pain. It scared the shit out of me.

The nuns also told us all about sin. There were thousands of sins, ones that you actually committed and ones you only thought about it. It really didn't make any difference whether it was real or imagined; if you did one or the other you were still going to spend some time in Hell or Purgatory for it.

There was a lot to remember. When the nuns weren't telling us how bad we were, or how our sins were going to take us to one of the fiery places, they were punishing us for infractions of rules. They had plenty of rules there at The Sacred Heart Academy. When you violated them the nuns came after you.

They had those long pointer sticks that teachers used to use, a sort of sawed-off pool cue with a rubber tip at the end. When we screwed up, the nuns would make us come to the front of the class and hold out our hands. Then they'd thrash them with their pointer sticks, sometimes until we were bleeding.

Man, those nuns were tough. From what I could tell from my short time with them, the Catholics seemed a cruel bunch. Sometimes I wonder if I'll ever be able to understand what it was all about and if I'll ever be able to forgive them for what they did to me and the other kids in my class.

Finally the school term ended and I was allowed out of that nun-run penitentiary of Catholicism. I re-entered public school that January.

My new school was Jefferson Elementary School, not very far from us in Lennox. Although The Redhead still scared and tortured me whenever she could, my life began to have some degree of normality to it. That March when I turned ten years old, Hank Messler bought me a used bicycle. Although The Redhead wouldn't allow me to ride it to school, I was allowed to ride it after class. I began to get to know my new neighborhood and I began to make some friends.

The Jefferson School was decent. It was a lot more relaxed than either the Catholic school or the reformatory and I got along with my classmates and did OK in my studies there. Still, every now and then The Redhead would get a wild hair up her ass and drive over to the school in the morning before I got there. She'd fill my teacher's ears with the same kind of lies she told the monsignor and the reform school administrator. I was bad. I was a thief. I was a liar, etc. Then when I'd get to school, I'd catch hell for these things I hadn't done. I'd get scolded or punished or kept after class. Then she began to physically abuse me.

She would beat me with sticks and tree limbs, with frying pans and pots over the head. Sometimes she'd come at me with sharp knives and slash at my arm and legs, cutting them up and leaving scars that are still there. Every so often she'd come at me with a small pairing knife and stick me in the side or in the belly.

On one particular day, The Redhead got so angry with me (for what I can't now remember) and she took a three-eighths inch piece of welding rod and came after me with it. She took the rod and wrapped it in a towel and started beating me with it. She beat me so bad that I went into spasms and convulsions. She stood there above me while I jerked around on the kitchen floor. She was laughing and smiling that maniac lipsticked grin of hers.

Then she saw that it was serious; that I wasn't faking the convulsions; that I was beginning to foam at the mouth. She scooped me up and put me in the car and drove us north into Inglewood where she took me to a clinic. The doctor treated me and talked with The Redhead while I waited. I could see they were having an argument. Then when that was over, the Redhead took me to a motel where we spent the night so Hank wouldn't see me. When I got home the next day, he did see the damage to me and gave The Redhead a strange look. By this time I'm pretty sure that Hank was on to her and her habits. I think he was starting to see that the woman that he'd gotten involved with was far from a normal woman.

Sometime that spring, The Redhead's bullet-holed green Model A got hit by an ice truck. It was broadsided by the truck and that green car was totaled. The Redhead claimed she was injured by the accident. She started walking with a limp and sued the ice company for damages.

The case dragged on for the rest of the summer.

When it was finally settled, The Redhead got a fair chunk of change out of the deal. She also wound up with an almost brand-new car. It was a 1936 Auburn Speedster Supercharger, a chrome yellow convertible with big silver exhaust pipes and tan leather interior. Now the woman who was hell on wheels was truly hell on wheels and she started blazing away on new trails now. Most of these trails led to other men.

It became obvious to me during the next school year when I was transferred to the El Segundo School down in Hawthorne near Hank's deli. We moved there from Lennox after The Redhead's settlement came through. We rented a bigger house down in Hawthorne. This one was three bedrooms instead of two, but it looked pretty much like the other bungalow we moved from. It was stucco, but this one was yellow, not brown. Maybe she got it because it matched her new car. Who knows? But pretty soon I became aware that The Redhead and her new hot rod were attracting a lot of men, and what was going on between them was pretty well out in the open.

When I would get home from school in the afternoon, the men would start coming around. Guys would pull up in cars. They'd say "Is your mother home?" And if I'd say yes, they'd say "Is she alone?" If I said yes again, they'd say "Tell her So-and-so is here."

Cops came by to see her. So did firemen, fishermen, servicemen, salesmen, and other men in suits.

Sometimes I went with her as she made her rounds in Inglewood, Hawthorne and El Segundo. There was a special Texaco station that The Redhead went to, and when she got there she'd get out of the Speedster and go and talk with the gas station manager privately, leaving me to sit and wait for her while the attendant filled the car with gas. Then when she and the manager had finished talking, she'd get back in her yellow roadster and away we'd roar.

I never once saw her pay for gas at that station, and I don't think that she and the manager were discussing the weather. Not with the way they were leering at one another.

Unlike Granny, The Redhead didn't have any problem with my going to the movies. In fact, she insisted that I go and see whatever I wanted to see. Usually they were westerns with John Wayne or Randolph Scott, or maybe I'd see Tarzan movies.

At least three times a week she'd haul me off to the show, driving me there in the yellow Speedster. When we got to the theater, the theater manager would come outside and The Redhead would get out of the car and go over and talk with him in the same way she did with the guy at the gas station. The manager would then call for one of the ushers and point to me sitting in the car. Then The Redhead would come out, open up the door, and say "Follow that usher and watch the show. I'll be back later." Then the manager would get in the car beside her and away they'd go.

I'd sit there in the movie house for hours—sometimes from four until ten—watching the same movie over and over again until the usher would come back in to tell me that my mother was waiting outside for me in the car.

When I'd get back in, we'd drive back to the yellow bungalow in Hawthorne. Hank would be sitting in the front room waiting for us. I could sense from his expression that he wasn't too pleased. He must have known what The Redhead was up to. Everybody else in the neighborhood sure did.

Kids and their mothers and fathers would talk about her and how wild she was. They'd talk about who she'd been seen with lately, and what they did together. One day at school a kid came up to me and said that his brother was sleeping with my mother. I hauled off and socked him in the jaw, breaking my hand when I did it. I told Hank that I hurt it falling off my bike.

I couldn't tell him the truth, and it was one of the only times that I lied when I was a kid. I guess it might have been some kind of misplaced pride or something on my part. What kid wants to hear something like that about his mother? But by the middle of that fall term I'm sure that Hank was aware of everything that The Redhead was up to whenever she went away at night.

Hank's mother sure was. She would come over to our house and visit us once in a while. She was a very nice woman named Belle, and she would sometimes take me and my mother out to lunch at the big Woolworth's department store over in Inglewood. They had a cafeteria in the store, and we'd go there and sit in one of the big leather booths and have lunch. The waitress would come over and bring menus and ask us what we wanted to eat. The Redhead would kick me or pinch me under the table and point to something expensive on the menu that she wanted me to order. It was often something that I didn't want, and when the food would come I'd pick at it for a while. Then the waitress would come and wrap it up for us and we'd take it home where The Redhead would heat it up and finish it later.

Once when we were having lunch with Hank's mother, The Redhead got up to use the bathroom or something. Belle leaned over to me and whispered "You didn't want that lasagna, did you, Claude?" I shook my head no. "Then why did you order it?" I gestured in the direction of The Redhead's place. "She told me to do it," I said. Hank's mom leaned over towards me and stroked my head. Then she whispered is my ear. "You'd better be careful of that woman, Claude," she said. "She's nothing but trouble and she'll hurt you if she can."

Right after Thanksgiving of that year, The Redhead showed up at school one day in The Speedster. "Get in," she said, "you're going back to see Grandpa and Grandma. Grandma's dying." I got in and away we roared, shooting up Hawthorne, turning right on Florence and heading east. When we pulled up to the big house, Grandpa was standing outside.

The Redhead and I got out and she went over and talked with Grandpa privately for a minute or two. Then she went back out to the car, hopped in, and burned out of there. Grandpa wouldn't let her inside. Her own mother didn't want to see her daughter even though she was dying.

Grandma had cancer. She was wasting away in the front bedroom, the one where I used to sleep that faced onto the front yard where the lemon and pepper trees were. There was a terrible odor that her disease gave off, and to this day I'll never forget that smell. It was like a freshly killed chicken that had sat too long without being cooked and had now gone rotten.

It was a horrible time. Grandma was suffering and in great pain from the cancer. Grandpa and I did all we could to make her comfortable, but it was pretty useless I could tell. I'd hear her moaning and whimpering all night long and I cried in my bed listening to her. I stayed there in my old home for about ten days or so. Then Grandma died.

Grandpa and I and Grandma's church lady friends buried her in the cemetery just down the road near Exhibition Park. Then we all went back to Grandpa's house and had a meal and visited. The Redhead was waiting outside down the street in her Speedster. When we finished, Grandpa walked me out. The Redhead leaned out and yelled to me, "Get in the car and come with your mother," she said. Grandpa leaned down and hugged me. "Good luck to you, Claude," he said. "I think you're going to need it." Then it was back to hell in Hawthorne.

I did whatever I could to occupy myself back then—anything that would keep me busy and away from The Redhead and her beatings and slashings and head-poundings. I got a job working at the Wonder Market down on Hawthorne Boulevard close to El Segundo. I peeled boxes and boxes of potatoes for Hank at his deli. On Sunday, I'd buy as many copies of *The Los Angeles Times* as I could and put them under my arm and go down to the Lockheed Airport to sell them to workers coming off the midnight shift.

I also got a paper route, delivering *The Los Angeles Herald* to houses in my neighborhood. That job didn't work out too well. When I went out to collect for the papers from my customers, I found that The Redhead had already beaten me to it. "What do you mean?" the customers would ask. "We already paid your mother." When my route manager came over to collect my collections, I made up some story to stall him until I got paid from Wonder Market and Hank's deli. The Redhead pretty much put me out of the newspaper business.

Sometime that winter I heard about The Soap Box Derby. I think it was Hank who told me about it. He saw an article in the paper announcing it and asked me if I wanted to race in it. "I sure would," I told him. "Well, fine then," Hank said. "I guess we'll have to build a car then."

We went to the big hardware store in downtown Los Angeles and bought the materials. We used light but strong alder wood for the frame, and even lighter wood panels for the body. We used ropes for the steering, and bought the other apparatus for the steering system; rods for the axles, and good stiff rubber tires for the wheels.

Hank and I worked on that race car all the time that winter. The days grew into weeks, and the weeks grew into months. Finally we finished the racer and painted it a shiny deep cherry red.

On race day Hank borrowed a friend's truck and drove it up with me. The Redhead took the yellow Auburn Speedster and got all dolled up and drove there by herself. She sure looked pretty. You never knew whom you might run into at a soap box derby, I guess she thought.

The race started on the Brea Mountain, on La Brea Boulevard up in the Baldwin Hills. It was a three-day-long race, and we ran it in heats, with the winner qualifying for the big race on Sunday. We looked on the chart they had posted and found what time my heat was scheduled to run that Friday. There were thousands of people there, and it was exciting being a part of it.

When my heat was announced, I was in lane four. The starter guy counted down with "On your mark, get set" . . . , then he fired his starter pistol. The next second we were flying down the hill, and the ground was just a blur below us.

Suddenly something happened. My beautiful red race car started flying apart. The left front wheel came off and I lost control of the car. I crossed over the lane marker and sideswiped the car next to me, taking it out along with mine. When our cars finally came to a stop, I looked down at the finish line a hundred yards away where I saw The Redhead. She was smiling and laughing.

Hank and I gathered up what was left of my beautiful red racer and packed the pieces onto the truck. On the way home, The Redhead insisted that I come with her in the Speedster. When I got in the car, she pulled something out of her purse and showed it to me. It was one of the cotter pins from my car. The Redhead had removed it, causing me to lose control of the car and smashing it into the car next to me. "This is what holds the wheel on, you dummy," she said. She laughed like mad all the way home.

So I started spending more and more time away from home. I'd go to the movies as much as I wanted and I started going up to visit my Uncle Clint in Inglewood up near the Hollywood park racetrack. Clint was a great guy, and some people who knew the Russell brothers and The Redhead speculated that I was actually Clint's son, not his brother Claude's. I don't know if I'll ever learn whether or not that's true.

We would hang out at his house on Fifth Avenue between Florence and Slauson and talk. Clint had worked with my father Claude when they both worked at Shaeffer's cafeteria and Clifton's Cafeteria in downtown Los Angeles when they were owned by the Russell family. Clint was a baker and he'd teach me how to bake; one time he took me to the plant where he worked and I was given a tour like the one I got at the Goodyear plant.

Other times I'd visit with a neighbor and his wife who lived down the street from us in Hawthorne. The neighbor was a truck driver for Pepsi, and sometimes on Saturdays he'd take me and a couple of my buddies with him on his route that took him to Hermosa Beach. He'd drop us at the pier there and we'd fish all day until he came back to fetch us at the end of the day and bring us back to our homes in time for dinner.

When school let out in June for summer that year I spent most of my time working and trying to save money. I bagged groceries at Wonder Mart, peeled potatoes for

The Punk, 1933

"This is the Punk, March 18, 1939." "The Apothecary," by Norman Rockwell. Printed by permission of the Norman Rockwell Family Agency, Copyright 1939, the Norman Rockwell Family Entities.

The Punk (left), 1943

The Punk in Santa Maria oil fields, 1947

"My first wife," 1947

Hank down at the deli, and sometimes made deliveries for him where I'd get paid extra and sometimes get a tip from the customer. Some weekends I'd go up to Inglewood to spend time with my Uncle Clint. He'd sometimes have some work for me too, cutting lawns or painting rooms and the like. He also taught me the basics of how to cook and bake. That's what the Russells were known for. They'd had a couple of restaurants in downtown Los Angeles, from way back before the Depression, and they did pretty well at the restaurant trade for a while.

When I was at home that summer I'd spend the evenings with friends of mine like Elton Agner or Billy Richmond, doing dumb kid stuff like gigging for frogs in a little creek not far from our neighborhood, down by El Segundo. Some evenings I'd spend time with Hank. We'd just sit and talk about things, or maybe listen to the shows on the radio. The ones we liked were *Amos 'n Andy, Charlie McCarthy,* and *The Battling Bickersons,* which was about a couple who were always fighting. Sometimes The Redhead would be home with us, but she didn't like the shows that Hank and I liked, especially not *The Bickersons.* She'd sit for a while puffing away on a Domino, then she'd roll her eyes and get up. "I'm going out," she'd say. Then we'd hear the Speedster fire up and back out of the drive, leaving us to ourselves. Where sent went, she never said, but sometimes she'd insist that I come along with her—as far as one of the theaters that is. Then it was the old routine with the manager and usher would come to tell me my mother was outside.

By now I was pretty well on to The Redhead's game and had figured out how to avoid getting on her wrong side and getting beat with a frying pan or hacked with a pairing knife. What I did was avoid her, obey all her orders, and say as little as possible. That seemed to work, most of the time anyway.

In September, school started back up again and I went back to enter fifth grade at El Segundo School. Pretty soon, the war broke out in Europe when Hitler invaded Poland. He was already famous and powerful by then, and all the kids in school made jokes about him and imitated him from the newsreels we'd see of him when we went to the movie theaters. We'd hold our fingers under our noses to imitate his mustache and talk and gesture and make the stiff-arm salute that he did. We'd try and talk like him too, even though none of us spoke German. We'd just make German-speaking noises and strut around doing the goose step. At home, I'd sometimes hear Hank and The Redhead talking about him and the war and whether or not America would get into it fighting the Krauts, the Japs, and the Dagoes as everybody called them back then. They were all allies in fascism, Hank said, along with Franco in Spain, and Hank said that they meant to conquer the whole world and make everybody else fascists too. Hank said that war was inevitable, whatever that meant, and I could see that he didn't think there was anything funny about Hitler and what he and his fascist buddies stood for.

Sometime that spring I came home from school one day and saw that Hank was dressed up in a Navy suit. He had gone down to the Navy office and enlisted. He was from Canada and he enlisted in America so he could later become an American citizen. Since he was a bright and educated guy, the Navy made him an instant officer. He was going away in less than a week, he told me. It scared me, thinking that I'd now be alone with The Redhead, without an ally in the house to protect me from her.

We had a big going away party for Hank. It was a warm Saturday night, and some of our neighbor friends came down to have dinner with us and say their good-byes to him. He shipped out later that week and now I was alone with The Redhead.

I wasn't alone with her for long though. One day as I was walking home from school, she roared up in her Speedster. She waited until I was alone, just like she did the first time I met her. She screeched the car to a halt in front of me and got out. She was all dolled up in a brand-new shiny green suit and she had a suitcase in her hand. "Here," she said, handing me the suitcase. "I'm going to New York." I took the suitcase from her and tried to think of something to say. Nothing would come out. Once again I was stunned speechless by her. "You know how to take care of yourself," she said. "You're a toughened up kid by now. You're eleven years old." Then she got back into her yellow hot rod, put it in gear, and roared away, leaving me standing there on the sidewalk holding a suitcase.

I wandered the rest of the way home in a complete daze. She'd done it again. When I walked in the house, thee was nothing left there, all the closets were bare and all the furniture was gone. I wandered through the house wondering what I should do, but I couldn't come up with an answer so I went out onto the front porch and sat down trying to figure it out.

About an hour later, my friend Elton Agner pulled up on his bicycle. He asked me what I was doing, sitting outside my house with a suitcase. So I told him, told him that my mom had pulled up and handed it to me and went to New York, "Jeepers!" Elton said. "Your mom just up and left for New York and left you here alone? Why didn't she take you with her?" I told Elton that I didn't have an answer, that I didn't have many answers when it came to The Redhead. Maybe she has friends there, I think I said. Maybe it was one of those pen pals whose letters she was always picking up from her private box down at the Inglewood post office.

I told Elton that I couldn't think of what I should do now. I couldn't go back to live with Grandpa, because Grandpa didn't live there anymore and I didn't know where he was living now since Grandma died. "Come on with me Claude," Elton said. "We'll figure out something."

Elton took me over to his house. It was a big, two-story Mexican adobe style thing on 139th Street near Hawthorne Boulevard, about ten blocks away from where I lived. He came from a big family, with seven brothers and sisters, and there was a big garage out back. We leaned up a ladder against it and went up onto the garage roof. Then he went back inside the house and told me to wait for him for a while. When he came back, he had a couple blankets and a pillow with him, and he also had a peanut butter and jelly sandwich and a half a quart of milk. "Here," he said, "it's the best I can do for now. We'll figure something out." I took the bedding and made myself a place to sleep. Then I ate the sandwich and downed the milk. A whole new life was beginning, and though I was frightened and didn't know where it led, at least I knew that it didn't include The Redhead.

For a couple of weeks I stayed up there on Elton's garage roof under the stars. He'd whistle for me in the morning and put the ladder up for me to climb back down and go to school with him, smuggling me out a hard-boiled egg, a crust of bacon, or a biscuit. Then we'd go to school, and afterwards I'd go back to work at the Wonder Mart. After awhile, his parents were aware of what was going on with me, and they'd sometimes invite me for dinner when they had enough to share. Then, one weekend, his father came out and asked me what it was all about, and so I told him. "Well, we can't have you living outside. Claude. Let's see what we can do."

By that end of that weekend Elton and his dad and I had built a little lean-to on the side of the garage and fixed up a proper bed with an old mattress and some sheets and a pillow with a little two-drawer kid's dresser where I could keep my things. It wasn't much, but it was home for me then during the rest of that school year.

When school ended, Elton's dad asked me to come into the house one night for dinner. He and his wife asked me what I planned on doing that summer and I told them that I'd probably just work at the Wonder Mart. Elton's dad told me that he'd talked to a friend of his and that this friend could get me a job working as a cook at a zinc mine he owned up in Death Valley. "It's not bad money, Claude," he said. "Fifty dollars a month, and room and board for free. But it's hard work." I told him that I didn't mind hard work; that I always worked hard, and he told me the job was mine.

Elton's dad wasn't exaggerating. The work was hard, the hours were long, and the summer sun in Death Valley was brutal. We'd start work at five, when it was still dark and cold, and then work all the way through until six, when it was sometimes 120 degrees. And if the heat and the work weren't enough, there were the snakes in the mine when I went in there. They were rattlers, at least a hundred of them, maybe more. When I walked into the mine entrance, I'd carry a stick with me so I could clear them off the timbers hanging overhead. They'd rattle at me for a bit and then they'd sink off to a corner and hide.

But it was all worth it. When the summer of 1940

ended, I had $150 saved and I was starting to get big in the chest and the neck and the thighs. I was no longer a puny little kid, and I had money in my pocket and a brand-new trade that could get me new jobs as a cook. I stayed with Elton for another two years and a half, living on smuggled sandwiches, occasional dinners at the table with his family, and living by my wits.

I worked every day after school at the Wonder Mart and I hustled newspapers on weekends at the Lockheed plant. That was also when I began my short career as a bootlegger. I'd get liquor from one of the guys that I worked with at the market and then take it back to the lean-to and divide it up into small jars that I'd sell to the neighbor kids on weekends. It didn't last long, but I was able to pocket a few dollars off it.

When I needed to have a note sent to school or have my report card signed, I'd take it to Elton's older sister Marie and she'd sign it for me. Not one of my teachers ever asked me about The Redhead, whom they all knew by then. I think the word was out that she'd gone to New York and left me alone, but nobody said a word about it.

I don't know how I made it through that period as well as I did. Just determination, I guess. I didn't want to quit, and I though that this was just another test I was being put through. Then, one day in December 1942, I was called down to the school principal's office. As I walked over there I wondered what I'd done to deserve having to go to the principal's office; it was always a bad sign of trouble coming your way when you got called down there.

When I entered, I found out that I was right. There were two L.A cops standing there waiting for me. "Are you Claude Russell?" they asked. I said that I was. "Well, Claude, we've come to take you home to your new house in Highland Park. Your mother wants us to bring you home." I was thinking to myself that home was anywhere that The Redhead wasn't. She'd trapped me again, and there wasn't a damn thing I could do about it.

They put me in the cop car and we stopped by the Agners' house. The cops went over to Elton's parents while I collected my few things from the lean-to. "Well, Claude, we'll miss you," they said. "Good-bye and good luck." I told the Agners thanks for all their trouble and asked them to say good-bye to Elton for me. They said that they would and asked me to come out sometime and visit them. I said that I would, and then I got back into the cruiser with the cops and we drove off.

We drove through Hawthorne and Inglewood and back through Los Angeles, driving down Florence, past near where Grandpa and Grandma and I lived. We turned left on Rita Avenue and came to a stop at a house just south of Gage. It was maybe half a mile from Grandpa and Grandma's house, maybe less.

The house was a little one-story wood frame thing. It was yellow, and in the driveway there was the yellow Auburn Speedster convertible. The door of the house opened, and The Redhead came strutting out of it, all dolled up and made up. "Go inside," she told me. Then she signed some papers that the cops had and flirted with them for a while. Finally, they left and she came back in. "I hear you're a cook now," she said. I told her yeah, that I had cooked at Mr. Agner's friend's zinc mine. "There's some pork chops in the refrigerator. Why don't you cook them for us?" It wasn't really a question. It was an order. If I knew what was good for me, I'd do it. So I did, and thus began another chapter of life with the Redhead.

She enrolled me at a new school, whose name I forget. She told me to get a job to help support the house, so I did. I didn't get one job. I got three. I worked at a kind of malt shop place called Fosselman's Dairy. I guess you could say that I was a soda jerk. I went to school from seven until noon. Then I'd start at Fosselman's and work there from 12:30 until seven. Then I'd go across the street to a bowling alley where I'd set pins from 8:00 until maybe midnight. Then I'd go home and get to sleep, and get up at 5:30 when I'd start my new paper route.

The Redhead hadn't changed her act one bit. I soon found out that she was doing my collections for me and leaving me in the same jam with my manager like she'd done before. Then she started coming by Fosselman's and the bowling alley to collect my weekly checks. She was unbelievable, a total thief. Finally after a few weeks of this, I told the managers of the dairy and the bowling alley that I wanted my checks myself and would pick them up on Thursdays after work. A sort of cat-and-mouse game developed with The Redhead and me as to which of us would get there first.

By early spring, I'd had enough. I told my bosses that I'd be leaving soon, and they understood what it was all about. The waitresses at Fosselman's passed a hat for me and asked all the customers to contribute to it too. I still had ten dollars from my savings left when I got off work that Thursday evening, they'd scraped another fifty together to add to my thirty-dollar paycheck. So, with ninety dollars to my name, I got on my bike and headed north, over the Ridge Route, heading to Bakersfield and then points north.

The Ridge Route was what we called San Fernando Road, and it ran straight up the San Fernando Valley from Los Angeles to the Grapevine near Gorman. On the first day I managed to get about as far as Lake Castaic, where I spent the night. The next day I got to Gorman, where I spent the night, sleeping at an old car wrecking yard. The next day, I started down the steep Grapevine, burning my brakes as I came downhill. The next day I finally made it to Bakersfield where I checked into a motel. I had a good long bath, washing the road grime and bugs off of me, then slept like a baby until noon the next day.

I went to a local second-hand store and sold my bike, getting five dollars for it. Then I went to the Greyhound bus station and bought myself a ticket to Portland, Oregon. The trip took three days, and by the time that I got there I was down to less than seventy dollars. Nobody on that bus asked me where I was going or why I was traveling by myself. They left me alone.

I rented a motel room for a week, while I felt out the city to see what prospects were available to me. They weren't as good as they were in Los Angeles, so I went back into the newspaper business, buying armloads of *The Oregonian* and selling them on the street.

I stayed in Portland for about three or four months, living on the street, sleeping in vacant cars, in city parks, and sometimes in a motel room when I could afford it. Besides the newspaper business, I also took odd jobs doing whatever was available. I mowed lawns, cleaned service station bathrooms, picked-up around construction sites. I did anything I could to keep alive.

I was just starting to get a feel for Portland, when the local police stopped me one day to ask me why I wasn't in school. I had no answer for them. Then they asked me where I lived, and I was just as vague about that. They took me down to the station and eventually wormed it out of me. When they found out I had run away from my mother down in Los Angeles, they sent me to juvenile hall for a few days. Then they put me on a train with half a dozen other L.A. runaways and a couple of armed guards.

At the Los Angeles police station, they notified The Redhead that they had picked me up in Portland and were sending me to juvenile hall.

When I went to court I appeared before Judge J. A. Scott. He was a noted juvenile judge and there's a statue of him in L.A., honoring him for his work in the juvenile justice system. Maybe he did some good, but from my experience, Judge Scott was a total asshole. He told me that he was going to send me back to live with The Redhead. This time I spoke up.

I told Judge Scott that I'd rather go to hell than live with that woman again. I told him that she was a liar and a cheat and a child abuser and that I was terrified of her and what she might do to me. Judge Scott sent me back to juvenile hall for a week to give me "time to think it over," as he put it.

I came back a week later to appear before him. Judge Scott asked me if I'd thought my case over and I told him that I had. "Well, are you ready to go back to your mother now?" I told him I'd rather be dead. He looked at me hard, and then he sighed. He looked through some papers for a minute and then he said I could pick one of three choices. He told me that I could go back to The Redhead or to a foster home, or he would send me to a correctional institution until I was twenty-one.

I told him that I thought there was a third choice. He looked down at the papers and said that the third choice was what was called a "minority cruise." A minority cruise was a thing that they had in wartime for kids who were over sixteen, but not yet eighteen. He said that he could send me on one of those but it depended on my age; there were two birth certificates for me, he said. One said I was sixteen, the other said I was fourteen. I told that the one saying I was sixteen was the right one. It wasn't true, so far as I could remember, but he did have a certificate saying that it was and he decided to accept it. A week later I got released from juvenile hall and went down to the L.A. County Courthouse to enlist in the Navy. Shortly thereafter I was shipping out to Port Hueneme for basic training. Pretty soon, I'd be a Seabee, shipping out for the South Pacific, and that's whole other story.

During the war and after it, when I went into the oil business, I was always so busy fighting or drilling that I never thought of The Redhead again. Then I started my own family and forgot about her, almost entirely. She was a memory that only crossed my mind occasionally. It stayed that way for ten years, from 1943 until 1953, then I got the news that Grandpa Von Strafer had died and that changed my luck. I was about to see the Redhead one last time.

The funeral for Grandpa was held up in Oxnard, near where I was living at that time. My uncle Clint came up from Inglewood and a few other Russells came up from L.A. as well. My wife's parents came up from Bell Gardens, down near L.A. and it was a bright sunny day and seemed as though it was going to be a pleasant ceremony. Then The Redhead showed up and that changed things for me.

All the old creepy feelings came back over me, all the old unpleasant memories. The beatings and knifings, the sudden arrivals and departures, the thievery, the lies, the hussy behavior—all of it came to life in me again.

Somebody from the family—Clint, I think it was—went over and talked to her for a few minutes. She nodded and didn't move. Clint later told me that he told her that she wasn't welcome inside the chapel. The family didn't want her there but that she could follow us out to the cemetery afterwards.

We drove out to the cemetery in single file with headlights on, the family cars following the hearse. The immediate family was seated close to the open grave on folding chairs. The minister said some words then all of us filed by the grave and tossed our flowers in after they lowered Grandpa's casket. I was talking with someone when I felt a presence behind me. I turned around and there was The Redhead.

She looked a little different now. Her red hair wasn't long, loose and wavy like it once was. Now she wore it in a short pageboy cut. She had also aged a little bit too, with lines starting to show on her face around the eyes and mouth. She was still smartly dressed and still smelled of perfume. And she wasn't alone either. She had a man with her. She brought him forward and introduced him to me, telling me his name and calling me her son. I forget what his name was but she introduced him as her husband, her seventh, I think. He seemed like a nice guy. He was a preacher. He was also two years younger than I. I shook his hand and he told his wife that he'd wait for her in the car. She held out a rose to me, forcing me to take it. I stood there with it my hand. I still hadn't said a word. Then she said this to me: "You know, Claude, I am your mother and you'll have to forgive me one day." I told her that I also had to take a shit every day but it wasn't something I necessarily looked forward to. Then I walked away, leaving her there. I didn't look back.

That was fifty years ago. I've never seen her since, nor have I ever heard whatever happened to her.

Fifty years is a long time to harbor hatred and resentment for someone, I know that all too well. But try as I may (and I don't very much), I haven't yet let go of it. The Redhead still haunts me, still troubles my dreams.

She still crossed my thoughts—even more now since I began writing this book.

For years I asked myself what had ever gotten into her to behave the way that she did. I asked myself what in the hell had possessed her to do things that she'd done to me. What had I done to deserve the kind of torture she used to practice on me? I really have no answers to those questions just yet. Not at this moment anyway. When I talk to my editor about this, he tells me that I maybe never will but that I might by the time that I finish the book. I don't particularly like to hear that because it seems that I might have to dig down deeper into those locked-away memories to draw out an answer. I have no way of knowing that just yet, but I guess I'm willing to look into it a little deeper if I have to.

What I do know and can say now is this: Ila Ona "Peggy" Baker-Russell-Messler-Whatever-Whomever-Whatever-Whomever-Whatever was my biological mother. Everyone also disliked her but her string of male suitors/husbands/conquests. She behaved badly, abused children and elders, and seemed to have no concerns other than her personal wants and needs.

That much is true, and I saw all of that. I sometimes wonder what it was that enabled me to survive that frightening time that I was left in her care, a care that expressed itself in torment and cruelty. I think about that only for a minute before the answer comes to me. The reason I was able to survive The Redhead was because of Papa and my first real family, the Velascos.

Four

Papa and the Velascos: Discovering My True Family

One day in the 1930s, Grandpa and I were out in the chicken coop, hiding from Grandma and sloshing down a bucket of beer. That's when I first heard about the man I call "Papa" and his family, the Velascos. Grandpa told me that they had raised me before he and Grandma had gotten a hold of me.

His mention was made in passing and I didn't take any great notice of it. Maybe it was because I knew by then that my family life was far from normal and this latest news from Grandpa didn't possess much shock value. I have no way of knowing now. I barely remember the incident. I just remember that Grandpa told me that when I was young I had lived with a Mexican family.

Then, in 1953, when Grandpa was dying of cancer, he told me about the Mexicans again. Grandpa was at his last address, out in Carson near Long Beach, where he was operating a kennel raising guide dogs for the blind. Grandpa was awfully sick when I visited him and he had that unforgettable smell of rotten chicken that has always signaled cancer for me. He asked me if I remembered the story about the Mexicans and I told him that I did.

"Their name is Velasco," he whispered. "That's all I

can tell you. I don't know where they are and I don't know much about them. I heard they were once a prominent family. That's all I know."

With that little bit of information I began my search for Papa. Eventually, six years later, I found him.

Maybe I should backtrack a bit here and go back to my time in the Navy during the war years.

After I enlisted and was sent to San Diego, I was transferred up to Port Hueneme where I underwent basic training. Then, in October of 1943, I was sent up to Oakland, California, where I was put aboard a ship heading for the South Pacific.

For the next two and a half years I served with the Seabees, the U.S. Navy's heavy construction crew. There were carpenters and bulldozer operators, engineers and crane operators, electricians, demolition experts and every other kind of construction tradesman you can name. And in the middle of all these highly skilled construction guys was me, this big fourteen-year-old kid.

I weighed 225 pounds by the time that I finished basic training. I had developed huge chest, arm and leg muscles and had a nineteen-inch neck. Despite my size, it was obvious to my fellow Seabees that I was still just a young kid. And so they gave me a nickname. Like all good nicknames it was one that stuck to me over the years. What they called me was "The Punk."

The war years were a different kind of hell. They sent us Seabees everywhere—to places like Saipan and Guam and to other tiny islands that didn't even have names and weren't on regular maps. They'd run us in by submarine and give us a small inflatable raft so we could put ashore. We were sent as advance parties so we could secure these areas that we'd later turn into docks and airfields after we'd gotten rid of the Japs who occupied them. There were battles we took part in to secure these sandy little stretches of South Pacific real estate. There were lots of battles, too many to recount right now. Besides that's best left alone for right now, and maybe that's a story that's best told elsewhere.

After the war I came back home to Los Angeles and went into the oil business. I started as a rigger with the Read Roller Bit Company. I was paid a grand total of nineteen-dollars a month to start. Six months later I was earning five-hundred-dollars a month. The oil business was still a pretty good industry back then.

I got married to a lovely young girl named Bea and moved in with her and her parents, living in a tent in their backyard in Bell, California—not far from Grandpa and Grandma's old house. Then we moved north from Los Angeles up to Ventura County where we lived in a little town called Orchid, near Santa Maria. Tom Yake, a guy that I was working with at the time, helped Bea and I get started. He helped us find a house up there and became friends with us during the early days of our marriage. Bea and I bought a little two-bedroom home with a G.I. loan and soon started a family.

I was on call seven days a week back then and worked at every major oil field there was in California. I worked at King City and San Ardo up in the Salinas Valley; Huntington, Long Beach and Wilmington down in L.A.; Murphy and Coyote and Lost Hills up in Kern County; and Ventura and Oxnard Plains in my now home county of Ventura.

I worked as a truck driver, bit peddler, and directional drilling operator for fifteen years until the oil business began to play out in the middle-fifties. Then I went into the trucking business full-time. It was while I was working as a trucker that my life took an unexpected turn that finally provided me the opportunity to meet Papa.

By the time I started as a trucker, my marriage was starting to break up. My wife was working at Bank of America back then and I was working full-time as a trucker, hauling loads between Los Angeles and Ventura. I was wondering what I should do about my crumbling marriage when an answer came to me unexpectedly.

I was driving back home to Santa Maria from L.A. It was rainy and late, near two A.M.,when I hit a wet patch and lost control of my company car. The car skidded and eventually flipped, rolling into a ditch and knocking me unconscious. When I awoke it was to the sight of a horribly disfigured man.

He was badly scarred and hunchbacked and his nose and a number of fingers were missing. I panicked and screamed, thinking that it was a bad dream. The man told me to calm down, that an ambulance was on the way. Then I looked and saw my arm—or what was left of it anyway. It was totally mangled and the bone was showing. It was hanging on by just a few shreds of flesh. I passed out.

When I woke up again, I was in the hospital in Ventura. There was nothing they could do to save the arm there so they flew me down to San Diego to Scripps Institute and the Navy Hospital. They had specialists there and if anybody could save the arm for me, it was those doctors, they said.

But the news in San Diego from the specialists was no better than the news I'd been given in Ventura. Bone and nerve specialists at these two different hospitals told me the same thing. I was going to lose the arm; they'd have to take it off, sooner or later, they said.

I went for later. I told these fine specialists that I

wasn't ready to lose my arm just yet. I asked them to do what they could to put my arm back together as best they could. Then maybe I could find somebody who could fix it. They looked at me, shook their heads and shrugged. So they put my arm in a gigantic airplane cast and sent me on my way. There didn't seem to be much hope for the arm, but I went on faith—or something like that.

Later that fall, I was heading south. I was driving from Ventura to Ensenada, Mexico. My marriage was over. My wife wanted a divorce, she'd found somebody else. Maybe it was somebody from her new circle of friends that she'd met at the bank. Maybe it was due to the long hauls that I had to make away from home. Maybe she wanted something different from a husband than what I could provide her. Maybe that was what made her attention wander elsewhere. Whatever it was didn't matter; all that mattered was that it was over. So I sold our place, our stocks and bonds, and all our other community property and split it with her right down the middle.

In 1959, I was a single man again. I was also unemployed and disabled and didn't know what was coming next other than that I was driving down to Ensenada, Mexico to meet a man named Gregorio Velasco. This was a man who I'd never seen before and had only heard about twice. The only reason that I knew he was in Ensenada was because I had hired private detectives and I had given them the name of Gregorio Velasco shortly after Grandpa died. When they got back to me they told me that a man by that name was running a restaurant down in Ensenada.

As I drove south through San Diego—my broken left arm in a cast hanging out the window—I thought about what I was leaving behind and wondered how my three young kids would make out in whatever new life their mother was leading them into. I thought about the oil business and wondered if it would turn around again. I thought about my possible return to trucking and whether I'd ever be able to drive again. I thought about my shattered left arm and whether I'd ever be able to use it again, or even if I'd be able to keep it.

I also thought about whether it was a wise thing for me to be coming down here to visit the Velasco family. I wondered what kind of reception I'd get from them. Call it worry. Call it concern. At any rate there was a lot on my mind and it seemed to magnify the closer I got to Mexico.

But a funny thing happened as soon as I crossed the border. Once I crossed over, I felt completely at ease. It felt like I was home. It was odd that I felt that way then because I'd only known Mexico from the occasional weekend blowout with friends from work. But when the detectives found Greg down in Ensenada, something started to grow in me.

Now here I was in Mexico, feeling like I had gone home again. And it was only later that I learned from Greg that Mexico had truly been my first home, because that's where Greg and his first wife Maria had taken me when The Redhead had given me to them. My first home, from four months to five years old, was on a ranch in Sonora.

I drove south on Mexican Highway 3. I drove through funky, filthy Tijuana and the pretty little beach town of Rosarita. Then down through El Descanso and El Sauzal. Seventy-two miles below the border I finally reached Ensenada.

It was another pretty beach town and it was then just a little city of maybe 15,000 people. I stopped at a gas station and asked if they knew about a restaurant called Velasco's. "Certamente, Señor," the attendant said and gave me directions on how to find it. I drove out to where he directed and saw big neon sign that said Velasco's over a fairly large building right on the beach.

I walked into the place and looked around. It was a very classy place and it was filled with people out for a night on the town. A waiter came over and showed me to a table. I ordered a Margarita and then asked the waiter if the owner was present. He said that he was and I asked him if I could speak to him for a minute. The waiter left and when he returned it was with a well-dressed man in his early fifties. "I am Gregorio Velasco," the man said in English. "I am told that you wished to speak to me. What is it that I can do for you, Señor?"

I told him that my name was Claude Russell, and that I was a truck driver originally from Los Angeles. Then I blurted it out. "I believe it was you who raised me when I was a little boy," I said. "From when I was a baby until I was about four or five."

The man's eyes glistened for a moment and his lip trembled. "Claudio?" he said. "Claudio, is it really you?" Then he threw his arms around me and embraced me softly so as to avoid hurting my broken arm. He kissed me on both cheeks and then he began to cry.

He called his family over and introduced me to them. "Amelia," he said to his wife, "look at our little Claudio. He's come back to us." For the rest of the evening it was a family reunion as Papa told me about his restaurant and his other businesses. He told me tales of his family and of the time that we spent together in Sonora when I was a little boy. We talked throughout dinner. The Margaritas were excellent and the steak and lobster dinner I was served was the best I've ever had—before or since. A mariachi band played and we talked and drank and ate and smoked cigars until the restaurant closed. Then Papa took me home with his family. I had the sense that I was almost whole again. I was home, in Mexico with my first, my real family.

For the next few days we visited and feasted. A *fiesta* was held in my honor and all the Ensenada bigwigs came to meet me and pay their respects. I was a guest of honor and the Velascos wouldn't think of my offer to stay in a hotel. "You are with your family again, Claudio," Greg said. "There's plenty of room here at our hacienda."

I learned from Papa that his life hadn't been any picnic either. Greg was born in Quartzite, California and carried dual citizenship as both a Mexican and an American. His father owned a ranch out in Sonora and Greg was helping him run it. One day, they were driving to town on a mountain road and were driven off it by a drunk driver. The injuries that his father suffered proved to be fatal and Greg blamed himself for his father's death. Greg was at the wheel when the accident happened. He promised his father that he would take care of his brothers and the family business when his father was dying. Then he left Sonora and moved back north to California.

Greg got married in California to a woman named Royale and was trained as a diesel mechanic in Los Angeles. Then he moved north with his wife to Stockton, up in the San Joaquin Valley, where he bought a little ranch. The ranch was located directly adjacent to a new freeway that was then being planned. Greg tried to get a loan on his property so he could construct a gas station; he thought he would make a fortune. But Greg couldn't get the bank to finance his proposal. Greg told me that he thought that the bank was prejudiced against him because of his Mexican background. Although I have no way of knowing if that was really the case, I do know that things like that were common in California back then.

So Greg sold the Stockton ranch and moved back down to Sonora where he took over his father's ranch and went to work for the American Canal Company. The ACC were then constructing a major water diversion project from the Colorado River, and the company hired Greg as a mechanic.

Papa and Royale had two little children by then. Greg was away during the week working on the canal project but he would return home on the weekends. One weekend, Greg returned home and found that his wife and children were nowhere to be found. He searched through the house and then began calling out their names. Finally his five-year-old son Pedro appeared. Greg asked the boy where his mama and sister were. The boy said he didn't know. Greg began searching the grounds of the ranch and noticed that the pail at the well had been lowered. He looked down into the well and thought he saw something. When he descended down the rope, he saw a small pair of legs. Elena, his seven-year-old daughter had fallen into the well and drowned.

When his wife finally returned the next day, Greg confronted her with her daughter's body and demanded to know what had gotten into her to abandon her children to care for themselves while she was away. What Greg told me was that she was out catting around. He divorced her, and then some years later married his second wife, Amelia, and moved back to the States for awhile, settling in Los Angeles and working as a diesel mechanic for a trucking company.

After our first few days of getting reacquainted in Ensenada and finding out about him and his life, Papa asked about my arm and how it happened. I told him the whole gory tale—about the late night run and the car flipping over and the disfigured but kind-hearted fellow who'd aided me. I told him about my time at the hospitals in San Diego and how the specialists there wanted to take my arm off and how I wouldn't let them. I told Greg that they told me that it was pointless, that I'd never be able to use my arm again. Papa listened patiently to my story until I had finished. Then he spoke. "I know a very good doctor in Tijuana," he said. "We will make an appointment and go up to see him. He is a brilliant doctor, one of the best in Mexico, and he specializes in cases such as this."

Two weeks later I was lying on an operating table at the doctor's clinic in Tijuana about to go under an anesthetic. My doctor was standing by with two nurses. His name was Dr. De la Plata, and he was a specialist in something that was then unpracticed in the United States.

Dr. De la Plata's specialty was bone-grafting. And Papa was right. Dr. De la Plata was brilliant. He looked down at me lying on the table and asked if I was ready. I said that I was and he put the mask over my face. He turned on the gas and I looked at the clock. It was eleven A.M. when I went under and Dr. De la Plata began the operation. When he finished it was 3:30 A.M. He and his team had worked on me for sixteen and a half hours straight.

Later I found out that this was typical with Dr. De la Plata. He was an ex-military officer who then became a surgeon specializing in the brand-new field of bone-grafting. His clients were mostly wealthy Mexicans and Americans who couldn't obtain this kind of treatment back home; that was how Dr. De la Plata made his living.

He also donated thirty hours of his valuable time per week, working with the poor.

A few days later Dr. De la Plata sent me home with Papa. He gave Greg some directions in Spanish and said that I must follow them religiously. "You will call me if you have any problems, Señor Russell," he said to me. "We will keep checking on you every day to make sure that the bone grafts are successful." I was still in the airplane cast, but at least I now felt hopeful. Maybe I wouldn't lose my arm. Maybe I'd be able to get some use out of it again, maybe.

Two weeks later, I was back in the operating room with Dr. De la Plata. The first bone grafts that he performed weren't working. He asked me if I was ready to go under again and I nodded yes. Eight hours later he had finished two new grafts. Then he sent me home with Papa and made us promise that I would follow his instructions to the letter.

When I got out of the arm cast I was sent by Amelia to a little town nearby and told to look up an old Indian man whose name I've long forgotten. The man was in his nineties then and I told him about my arm in broken Spanish until he nodded that he understood. The old Indian gave me herbs and treated my arm with balms and oils and the like. As he was doing this, his young great-grandson was watching and listening while the Indian explained what he was doing. The Indian told me that he didn't want to see his ritual medicinal powers vanish and so he was training his great-grandson in the healing arts. He also told me about another Indian who was a traveling herb salesman and when he was expected to be in Ensenada. Greg was able to make contact with him and he regularly stopped by the Velasco hacienda to drop off the herbs we'd ordered. They seemed to help. I was willing to try anything if it would help save my arm.

For the next eighteen months I was in physical therapy seven days a week. I'd exercise the arm as I was directed to by the therapists and would squeeze a hard handball to rebuild the frayed nerves. I went to the beach every day during that time and I would swing my arm while I walked—sort of like power walkers do today. It hurt like hell. When I got to the beach I'd dogpaddle out beyond the waves to where the ocean was calm and tread water for as long as I could, using my arms to help keep me afloat. Then I'd body surf back in again.

Over time I could tell that the arm wasn't just getting better, it was actually getting strong again. My arm muscles started developing. The dexterity in my fingers was improving. The numb feeling was staring to go away. The therapists worked the arm and massaged out the muscle adhesions. I was finally getting healed, and I needed to because as soon as I was able to move around normally again Greg told me he had a job for me. He wanted me to run the restaurant during the day.

My only experience in restaurants was from before the war—at Hank Messler's deli in Hawthorne, at Fosselman's Dairy in Highland Park, and in that rattlesnake-infested zinc mine out in Death Valley. Nothing had prepared me for anything like Velasco's, which was then one of the best, if not the best, restaurants on the Baja coast. I hardly spoke any Spanish back then, but that didn't matter to Papa. "You'll learn," he said. "You'll have to learn. It is *absolutamente necesario*, Claudio."

I'll tell you this: Velasco's was one hell of an upscale operation, and Papa was totally hands-on when it came to running his show. He had a high volume of business back then, and the restaurant could accommodate about 400 people in its many rooms. Papa took great pains to make sure that our food came from the best available sources. Fishermen would come in with their fresh catches and we'd buy from them right off the boat. They'd bring in lobsters and crab and squid and abalone. They'd bring in tuna, shark, yellowtail and swordfish. And there were a couple of boats who'd bring in Tuana, a fish that came all the way from China which then would spawn in the Colorado River. The Tuana were huge fish—from 300 to 400 pounds each—and they had the biggest scales on them that I'd ever seen, about the size of a half-dollar they were.

Poor people—farmers and peasants—would also come in with things to sell that Greg would buy direct. Some of them would bring in quail that they'd trapped; some brought in game hens they'd bred. Greg and I would go to Tijuana where we'd buy our freshly slaughtered beef, which was then the best beef available on either side of the border. The butchers would send it down to us in refrigerated trucks and Papa would store it properly, marking it for when he felt it was at its prime for serving to customers. Then, once a week, we'd drive up to San Diego in Greg's big blue Pontiac where we'd buy butter and cheese and other dairy products that were better and cheaper than what was available in Ensenada.

About once a month Greg would prepare a huge barbecue. He had a pit dug in the ground filled with hot coals and we'd barbecue the meat in it for two or three days, turning it from time to time and basting it with Greg's special barbecue sauce. Then we'd have a *fiesta* for three or four days and all the Ensenada high rollers would attend along with the poor people who were also great friends of Greg's.

The Margaritas flowed without end and the laughter

never stopped as the mariachis played until dawn. At one of those fiestas I thought to myself, *This is really the good life, and Greg and the Velascos are showing it to me.* I was happy and healthy again, at home in Ensenada.

During that time that I was convalescing, Greg's second wife, Amelia, used to go to church every day and pray for my complete recovery. She had bought a small silver arm from one of the Indian medicine men and she would place it on the altar and pray for my shattered arm. When the arm had healed enough to the point that I knew it would be useful again I asked Greg for some time off and flew over to Mexico City. I wanted to go to Our Lady of Guadalupe Cathedral. I was going there to pray.

It was a huge and beautiful cathedral located in the center of the booming city near the Zocalo and there were hundreds of other people from all over the world. They were there to make offerings and to say prayers for healing or thanks just like I was doing. I prayed for an hour or so and then I went up to the altar and placed my offering on top of it. It was a gold-plated arm that I'd had an Indian artisan make, similar to the one that Amelia had. I went back to my pew and stayed a couple hours more. When I left the cathedral, I was empty-handed. I had left my gold arm on the altar. My flesh-and-blood arm was fully functional again. It had healed completely.

While I was down in Ensenada I found that I liked it well enough to move there—or at least buy some property there. Greg and I formed a company based on shares and divided the shares between us according to how much each of us had invested.

Another of our partner/shareholders was a friend of mine from Ventura, a guy called Louie Levine. Louie went up to Tecate to the San Valentin Ranch, one of the finest wine-producers in Mexico. With Louie we bought one of the San Valentin properties called Estero's, which was a beautiful parcel along the beach in Ensenada just north of Papa's restaurant. We thought we had made a smart investment and we were encouraged when other investors followed our lead into El Estero, including a former Mexican president.

But our dream turned sour on us. The former Presidente had bought all the property but our little spit of land, and he died before the deal was formally completed. The *federales* then came down and took over the property and squatted there for eight or nine years. Condominiums and a tennis court were constructed. Then they started building on our property, investing a total of about fourteen million dollars down there in El Estero. We tried the old Mexican "*mordida*" (bribe) method of settling our claim, but to this day we're still in limbo on it. Perhaps that's something that I can help the Velascoes resolve for Papa and me whenever I get down to Ensenada.

During my years with Papa he told me much more about his life and times. He told me how he had gotten a hold of me from The Redhead. She had heard from friends of my actual father, Claude Russell, that they were a good family, and when she left my father, she took me to them and said that I needed a home. They agreed to take me in and she told them she'd come back to claim me when she was settled.

Papa also told me of his life in California, where he was born in a town called Quartzite on the California-Arizona border. And he told me of the Velasco family and of their history and how they had come to Los Angeles.

When I was with Greg in Ensenada he had an old chest full of family archives and he would show me documents from them dealing with his family and the land grants they'd been given in the New World. He told me that his family had come from northern Spain, and that they had converted to Islam after the Moorish invasion in the ninth century. The Velascos prospered in Spain under the Moors, but were the chased out of Spain during the Spanish Inquisition. He told me that the Velascos had to sneak across the country to avoid the brutal Catholic inquisitors, and that they finally made it to the Canary Islands where they reconverted to Catholicism. It was the age of Exploration back then, with all the imperial countries of Europe carving up the New World into spheres of influence. The Velascos saw no future in Spain and decided to try their hand in the New World.

Greg told me that the first Velascos had landed in what was then the Spanish colony of Mexico sometime in the 1500s. He said that the family had been given a large parcel of land somewhere in Mexico City and that they built a large mansion there. He showed me pictures of it and it was indeed a palace. Papa said that the Velascos had later moved to a large holding in Sonora and that they then went north to Los Angeles where they helped establish the city. The Spanish crown had then rewarded them by giving them a large land grant, and when Mexico successfully rebelled against Spain, the Mexican government had given them a new grant to the same lands. Greg said that the Velascos had held on to it until the middle of the nineteenth century when the U.S. government took over California from Mexico in 1848.

That was what Greg told me. It was also what he showed me, producing the documents from that large trunk. There were names and dates and grant titles and all such like in that chest, but now they are gone.

During the spring of 2003, when Greg's health was

beginning to fade and his body was ceasing to function, I called down to his house in Ensenada and tried to speak with him about how I could obtain copies of the documents. Papa could barely talk and he told me that he didn't know where they were. His wife told me essentially the same thing. So, with little else to go on other than the stories he told me, I hired a researcher to go down to Los Angeles to see if there was anything to substantiate Greg's stories of the Velascos and the grants and their settlement of Los Angeles.

My researcher spent a few days at the UCLA Special Collections Library and went through all the material available there that had to do with land grants in the Los Angeles area and how the city was founded. At the end of his second day of research he called me and gave me some bad news. There was plenty of material on the land grants given by both Spain and Mexico in the Los Angeles area, he said, but nothing in it mentioned the Velascos. He said he had one other source left in Los Angeles that might be useful and said he'd call me at the end of the next day after he'd finished his research. When he did, it was with good news. He had found documents that helped establish Greg's stories as factual.

In a book published by The Historical Society of Southern California on the early history of Mexico and California, there is a letter dated April 6, 1594. The letter was addressed to the King of Spain and it was from the Viceroy of New Spain, a man named Don Luis de Velasco.

The letter was from the Viceroy of New Spain, Don Luis de Velasco, and it was addressed to His Majesty, dated at Mexico, 6th April, 1594. Here is what the letter says:

In a paragraph of the letter, which on the 17th of January,

> 1593, Your Majesty ordered to be written to me, it is ordered that a survey and demarcation of the harbors to be found and from these islands [the Philippines, author's note] be made, with a view to the safety of the ships which come and go; and a ship and money being necessary for this purpose, or, at least permission to engage in ventures now prohibited by Your Majesty, in such a manner that the gain would compensate the labor, the ship *San Pedro* was bought, in which the exploration might be made on the return voyage, provided that the ships, which sailed last year, or some one of them, which sailed last year had failed to do this; and I ordered the navigator, who at present sails in the flag-ship, who is named Sebastian Rodriguez Cereno and who is a man of experience in his calling . . . and I wrote to the governor [of the Philippines, author's note] that he should allow him to put on board the ship some tons of cloth in order that he might have the benefit of the freight-money, and I caused him all that might be needed for the purpose, and concerning what he may do I shall advise Your Majesty in due season.

That seemed pretty impressive to me. This guy Don Luis de Velasco was the Viceroy of New Spain, the land that became Mexico.

Then, in a couple of other books, my researcher found material relating to the founding of Los Angeles, including two accounts of a man named Jose de Velasco y Lara. This man was one of the original forty-four settlers who founded the city back in 1781. Quoting from an article by William Mason and Roberta Kirkhart Mason titled "The Founding Forty Four" published in *Westways Magazine* in July 1976 there is this account of Velasco y Lara:

Jose de Velasco y Lara was an accountant and administrator for various haciendas in western Mexico. He married early, but did not get along well with his wife, and they eventually separated. He moved to Sinaloa where he worked for a time at some of the larger estates. He became involved with a young Indian woman of Sinaloa, . . . whom he impregnated. On hearing that his wife had died, he married his mistress in order to legitimize the baby. Not long after his marriage he heard that it was not his wife but her sister-in-law who had died, and that he had gotten a garbled report from friends. A rumor that his brother-in-law was searching for him prompted Lara, as he was now known, to enlist in the Riviera Expedition [the expedition that founded Los Angeles, author's note] thus avoiding his brother-in-law and probable legal consequences. In California, Lara pretended illness, so he said, to avoid sleeping with his wife. Father Juniperio Serra, after some correspondence about the case, called him to Monterey from Santa Barbara, where Lara was living, for a hearing. Lara explained his situation and was sent back to Nayarit, presumably to rejoin wife number one. He never returned to California.

When the researcher sent the material back to me there were a number of documents that I recognized from Greg's old box. There was a handwritten account of the departing settlers Mesa, Lara (Velasco) and Quintero that I remembered Greg having a copy of. There were accounts of the Spanish and Mexican land grants published in the book *Ranchos of California* by Robert G. Cowan. This book mentions three grants, one of which might be the one that Greg was referring to back in the late 1950s during my time with him in Ensenada.

There was the Jabonera grant—"somewhere within the City of Los Angeles"—which had been "granted to Santiago Martinez and 20 New Mexican families" who asked for it in 1843. But that grant was too new; it was from the Mexican era, not the Spanish era when the Velascos first arrived in the New World.

A more promising possibility was the San Rafael grant between Arroyo Seco and the Los Angeles River that had been granted to Jose Maria Verdugo et. al. in 1784. But this grant was made too late for it to correspond to the facts at hand. If Velasco y Lara had left Los Angeles in 1782 to return to Mexico, he couldn't have been one of the et al's mentioned in the San Rafael grant.

The most promising possibility turned out to be the San Antonio grant from 1814. This grant had been given "to the soldier Antonio Maria Lugo . . . whose parents hailed from Sinaloa" (in the Mexican state of Sonora, author's note).

Lugo's grant also included a number of et al's, and the location of the grant was between Lynwood, Bell, Montebelo and Marywood. This was the area right near Grandpa and Grandma's house on 69th and Converse. The time frame was also a good possibility because I remember Greg telling me that it was his great-grandfather who had been given the grant, and this time frame would correspond to the dates that Greg said his great-grandfather was in Los Angeles. I also remember Greg telling me that his great-grandfather was running a herd of 10,000 cattle on third and Spring Streets in what is now downtown Los Angeles. This location is just up the road from where the San Antonio grant was located.

Greg also said that from what he remembered, his family was grazing their herd up in the Hollywood Hills during the middle of the nineteenth century. This also corresponds to what my researcher had found. It was common practice back then during the early days of Los Angeles to allow ranchers to graze and water their cattle on whatever unsettled lands they found appropriate for that purpose. Cattle for meat, tallow, and cowhides was then one of early Los Angeles' main cash producers.

Looking through all these documents was confusing. It was especially so for me given my Alzheimer's condition and failing memory. So I called my editor in Eugene, I told him what I'd been sent and I asked him what I should do about it.

In mid-June of 2003 he came out to see me and we looked over all the material that I'd been sent. "This is interesting stuff, but it's still inconclusive," he said. I asked him what I should do next and he referred me to another researcher in Sacramento who might be able to help. I called her and she said that she'd get back to me when she'd come up with something, *if* she came up with something, she said. I thought about what else I might do and called down to Papa in Ensenada, it was almost impossible to understand him. He was obviously failing; he was getting much worse, his wife said. "I don't think he has much left to fight with, Claudio," she said. "I will let you know if there is any change in Gregorio's condition."

I thought about what I should do and couldn't come up with much. So I decided that there wasn't much left for me to do but to go to Ensenada and visit Papa one last time. I wasn't going there to try and pry something out of Greg on his deathbed, or to see if I could find out where the documents relating to his family might be. I was going there because it was time for me to go there. I wanted to pay my last respects to the man who had raised me from when I was a toddler. I wanted to say good-bye to Papa.

Five
Going Back to Papa and Ensenada

The news had been bad throughout the spring. It had all been bad—for me, for Papa, for my editor, for almost everyone I knew. For me, I had bad health problems, with one seizure, with Alzheimer's off and on that kept me from getting much done on the book, and with my cancer acting up. I was hospitalized for the cancer and had three tumors removed by my doctor here in Florence. One of those tumors was particularly nasty, and it took the doctor three separate operations in order to remove it fully.

For Papa, it was even worse. His stomach was deteriorating and he was on a soft food diet of baby food, mashed potatoes and gravy, and the like. Then they removed all his teeth. He had a woman doctor up in Tijuana, and Greg kept going up there to see her, hoping she would be able to do something to restore his vision, which was almost gone now. He had cataracts in his eyes which he wanted the doctor to remove, and Greg wanted desperately to be able to see again. The doctor humored him, giving him drops and making excuses of why she couldn't operate. Miguel, one of Greg's sons-in-law, told me that she wouldn't operate on Greg. He was too old, she told him, and Papa might not survive the operation.

When I called Greg in June, he could hardly talk. His son-in-law told me that they didn't think Greg would be around much longer. "He's very weak, Russ," they told me. "It could be any day now." I called back at the end of June and told them I'd be down in a week. Papa got on the phone and I told him the same thing, but I wasn't confident that he understood me.

On July 9, 2003, a friend of mine picked me up at my trailer and took me to the Greyhound bus station here in Florence. Originally, I was planning on going down to Ensenada with my editor, who would drive me there in his car. But then he called me in late June to tell me that he couldn't get away for ten days, and so I decided to take the Old Grey Dog.

It was 2:30 when I boarded the bus, bound from Florence to Oakland. From there, I would change to another bus that would take me to Los Angeles. Then I'd have to switch to another bus that would take me to San Diego. Then a friend of mine who lived there was going to take me down to Ensenada, where I was planning on staying for a week or ten days depending on Greg and his condition.

The trip down to Oakland was along the coast route, and I thought I'd take advantage of the long trip to do some reading that my editor had given me the last time he was in Florence. He'd brought me three books on early childhood development by psychologist/writers who are supposed to be experts in their field.

The trip to Oakland took us fifteen hours to complete, and I was able to do a fair amount of reading. I read the excerpts from the three books that my editor asked me to look at and didn't find anything that seemed to apply to me. The idea was that these books would give me some kind of clue of how young children learn about things during the time from their birth up until age five. There was stuff about "bonding" and "learning by imitation" and "emotional milestones" and stuff like that. I think my editor thought that I might find something in them that applied to what I had learned during my early years with Greg that helped me deal with The Redhead and Grandma and her holy-rollers.

The more that I read, the less it meant. People from my generation and background don't use words like "bonding" and "traumatic childhood experience" and all the others that I read in those books. I appreciated what these books were about, and how it *maybe* might apply to me, but I didn't see that it did. Perhaps there is something to these psychologists' theories that does apply, and that young babies do learn about life and how to deal with it in their very early years from watching the adults around them. But to me, it's really a lot simpler than that.

Adults taught me everything that I learned in life, and that includes the good, the bad and the ugly. As I wrote earlier, my entire life from childhood on was spent with adults, at least the parts of it that I can remember. There were Grandma and Grandpa in Florence, California, The Redhead in Lennox and Huntington Park, the Seabees in the South Pacific, and Greg, when I was with him in Ensenada. I'm sure there is something to the fact that the love and support that he and his first wife showed me did help me deal with all the difficult things that I later went through, but I have no recollection of it, and psychological terms like those in the three book excerpts that I read are almost a foreign language to me.

Perhaps it's just that I come from a different generation, our main preoccupations were survival, then work, then personal responsibility. The stuff in the books was all theory, and I'm afraid I don't have much use for theory. It's too late in my life to try and refigure it as a psychologist might. I'm near the end now and I'm afraid I just don't have the time to be re-educated to a new way of seeing things. The one that I have works fine for me, and what little time I do have left I'd like to spend it in more enjoyable ways than trying to find psychological explanations for how I turned into the man that I became.

At least the reading distracted me from the boredom of the fifteen-hour long journey down the coast in a bus that stopped at almost every wide spot along the highway. The company was nothing to write home about either: low-lifes and losers and poor people on the move. We got in to Oakland at about 7:00 in the morning, and then I boarded an inland-bound express bus to Los Angeles at 7:00 and got there at about 2:30. In L.A., I was frisked by a policeman, who found a pocket knife on me. I'd had that knife for maybe fifteen to twenty years, and it was almost like an old friend. The policeman said that he had to confiscate it and he did. It was a bad sign of what was to come on my trip to Ensenada.

I finally arrived in San Diego in the evening. It was still light and I grabbed my bags and went right next door to the bus station where there was a bar in The Pickwick Hotel. I called my friend, Fred Kaiser, an old truck-driving buddy of mine, and asked him to pick me up. After a day and a half of riding The Grey Dog, where they don't allow drinking. I was more than ready for a cocktail or two. I was on my second brandy and Coke when Fred came through the door. He sat down and we talked for a while. I told him why I was heading down to Ensenada. "I'm writing a book," I told him. "Am I going to be in it?" he asked. I told him "No, I decided to keep the assholes out of it." Fred laughed. Then he and I had another round and then we left for his house out in Lemon Valley.

Fred and I have known one another for something

close to forty years, from back in my trucking days when he was also a driver for one of the companies I was driving with—Humble Oil, I think. He and his wife, Kathy, and BB and I used to spend a lot of time together when we weren't working and he'd come up to Florence, Oregon to visit me there. I had some personal business to take care of in San Diego before I went down to Greg's, and Fred had agreed to drive me around while I took care of it. I thought it would take me a day or two at max, but I wound up staying with Fred for nearly a week.

The business that I had to take care of in San Diego was related to BB's daughter Linda Graybar, my step-daughter. She's about fifty-three now, and has been in and out of mental institutions for almost twenty years. She had volunteered for a government drug research program back in the late sixties when she was eighteen years old. I don't know what drug it was that they were testing, but it must have been a powerful one. She's never been entirely sane ever since then. I wanted to make sure that her needs were entirely taken care of before I went down to see Papa.

Linda had been in a hospital in Lakeside, a town just outside of San Diego. I called the hospital to check on her condition. They asked me if I was a blood relative of Linda's, and I told them that I wasn't. "Well, Mr. Russell, if you're not a blood relative then we can't tell you anything. We can't even tell you if she's here or not." Although I was angry at what I'd been told, I decided not to say anything about it. I know how bureaucracies and institutions work these days; there's no point in battling them. They beat you on technicalities every time.

The next morning I asked Fred if he would take me downtown, and for that whole day I did nothing but go from one office building to the next, trying to locate Linda.

I went to the police station, to the Sheriff's office, to the courthouse. It was no dice at every one of them. They couldn't tell me anything because I wasn't a blood relative.

The next day I got on the phone and did what I could to track her down. Eventually, I was able to get hold of Linda's caseworker from the Welfare Department. She wouldn't tell me anything either, but she said she would talk to her boss and see what she could do to help me. She suggested that I call back the next day.

When I called her the next day she said that she had some good news for me. She said that Linda would talk to me over the phone and that we could all speak together via a conference call. She told me to wait by the phone, and she would get back to me within an hour.

The phone rang about thirty minutes later and the caseworker and Linda were on the line. I asked Linda how she was and she said that she was OK. I asked her if she needed anything where she was and if there was anything I could do for her. She told me that she didn't need anything and it wasn't wise to send her anything because the people at the hospital would steal it. I asked her if she wanted me to come to the hospital and visit her. "No, Russ," she said. "It's not a good idea and it will only upset me. I'm OK here," she said. I asked her if she wanted me to send her some personal items that she might need, a bra, some new panties, cosmetics, things like that. "It'll only get stolen," both she and her caseworker said. "Isn't there anything I can do?" I asked the caseworker. She told me that there wasn't, and I said goodbye to Linda.

The next day I asked Fred to drive me over to The Neptune Society and I made arrangements with them to take care of Linda's remains and ship her ashes back to

Florence, Oregon where she will be laid to rest along with her mother and me.

The next day Fred and I got good and drunk and talked about old times in the trucking business. Then Fred's wife, Kathy, came home from her out-of-town insurance job in Irvine, California and made us all a fabulous dinner. Linda was finally taken care of, and I know that BB would appreciate that.

The following morning, Fred and I got into his Ford 3/4-ton pickup and headed out for Ensenada. We came down the coast through the old town that I once knew so well and made the trip in two and a half hours. North of Ensenada, where the road forks, we took the road to the left that heads up to Greg's house that sits on a hill that the locals call Chapultepec. The house is high enough so that it overlooks the Bay of Ensenada. We were just pulling into Papa's drive when I saw a sight that scared the hell out of me. There was an ambulance parked outside, and to white-uniformed attendants were going into the house.

A moment later, I saw the ambulance guys emerge with somebody on a stretcher. It wasn't Greg, it was Socorro, his third wife. A moment later, his son-in-law Miguel came out of the house to let me know what was happening.

Miguel said that the ambulance was taking Socorro up to Tijuana where her doctor was going to operate on her for problems caused by a varicose vein infection. "For a minute there, I was scared to death," I told him. "I thought that the ambulance was here for Papa." Then Miguel told me the bad news; that Papa was going into the hospital, too. "Manuel and I will be taking him out in a minute, Claudio," he told me. "We have to take him out to the airport. We've chartered a plane for him to be taken up to Mexicali. I don't know if he'll ever be able to make it home again, but I told him you were here and he has some things that he wants to tell you."

I was stunned. I thought I was going to pass out and I was getting dizzy, so I walked over to the yellow stone wall along the driveway and waited for Manuel and Miguel to bring Papa down. A few minutes later they came down the stairs with a big stretcher carrying Papa on it. He motioned for me to come over to him. I did, and he gripped my hand in a firm handshake. Then he spoke:

"I have heard from Socorro and Miguel that you are writing a book, Claudio," Papa said in English, "and they told me that you have come down here to find out more about me and my family and how you came to be with us. I will tell you what I can."

Much of what Greg told me didn't make much sense, but I was able to learn a few things about my early days that I had come down here to find. Greg told me that The Redhead had brought me to his first wife, Royale, and him in July of 1927, and that she had met the Velascos through a friend of hers. He also told me that I was only with him and Royale for three years, not four, and that I lived with them in their ranch house in Sonora until Grandpa and Grandma learned where I was and agreed to adopt me. He also told me that the documents were no longer in his possession and that he had no idea where they were. Then he gripped my hand and shook it hard again. "I'll keep the furnace door open for you, Claudio," he said and winked. Then his sons-in-law loaded Papa into an SUV and drove off

Miguel came over to me and said a few words and asked me to close the gate behind me when I left. Before I did, I went back over and sat along the wall and made some notes.

"Here I was," I began, "sitting on a wall at Papa's little salmon-colored *hacienda* up on Chapultepec, looking out on the Bay of Ensenada, which I've come to know like the back of my own hand. They've just loaded Papa and Socorro off to different hospitals, so I won't be staying down here for ten days, like I originally planned. I tried to talk with Greg, but he didn't make too much sense and could only give me a detail or two. At least I now know how old I am. I'm seventy-six, not seventy-four, like I always thought I was. I tried to talk to Miguel and Manuel, too, but they were too upset to give me much of anything."

Fifteen minutes later, I closed the gate behind me and Fred and I drove off, heading back to Lemon Valley. I was disappointed that I only had but a minute or two with Papa, but I'm glad that I did and was able to say goodbye and look him in the eye one more time and share a laugh with him about the furnace. There's nothing left for me to do here in Ensenada on this trip. The El Estero thing still isn't resolved, but it's still in court. I'm sure attorneys can take care of it, probably over the phone.

There was so much that I wanted to say to Papa, so much I still wanted to learn. Greg gave me more guidance and wisdom and love than anybody I've known in my life with the possible exception of Grandpa. I am proud to have known him, and happy to have loved him and been loved by him. Papa put me on the path of life that I'm on, and I know I'll never stray from it. Looking back over the years that I spent with him, I can say that it was a great honor for me to be part of his life and family.

When Fred and I got back to his house in Lemon Valley, we told Kathy about the trip, and I told her that I doubted if I'd ever see Papa alive again. The trip had taken more out of me than I thought it would, with all the drama about Linda and then arriving there in Ensenada to see Greg and Socorro being taken out of the little salmon-colored hacienda where I had spent so much time as part of the Velasco family. "What will you do now, Russ?" Kathy asked me. "I don't know, go back home to Florence, I guess," was my reply. But I still had one stop left to make, and that was to see my daughters up in Orange County.

On Monday, July 14, 2003, Kathy drove me up to Irvine, where I checked into a Travel Lodge. I called my daughter Linda at her place of business and told her that I was in town for the night. She and her husband, Ken Hood, own a painting and powder coating company called KENLEN SPECIALTIES out in Fountain Valley where my two other daughters Becky and Paula work as well. Becky said that there was a nice little Chinese restaurant at the Travel Lodge and that she and Paula, and Paula's husband, Kenny would come and meet me there. Then I lay down and rested for the rest of the day.

That evening, around seven or so, the phone rang. It was Becky, calling from her cell phone. She said they were nearing the freeway exit and would be at the restaurant in ten minutes. I got up, washed my face, combed my hair, and put on a clean shirt. When I walked in the restaurant, Becky waved me over. Paula, the youngest, was ill with asthma and couldn't make it, they told me.

We talked about everything about Linda's business and how the enviros were trying to shut down the KENLEN plant. They said it was producing toxic chemicals that were bad for the environment and they've been trying to close it for awhile now. We talked about BB's daughter, Linda; about my trip to Ensenada to see Papa; and about how I was coming with my book. I told them that things were OK with me, but that I was upset by what happened with Linda Dunbar, and that the visit to Ensenada was a great disappointment to me.

"Well, maybe this will help a little bit," said Linda.

She reached into her briefcase and pulled out a newspaper clipping. It was from the oil field Shriner's club newspaper, whose name now escapes me, and it was dated from 1964. In it, there was a big article about "The Punk's Night," which was held at the Converse Ranch on West Mountain in Santa Paula. Until Linda pulled out the clipping, I had entirely forgotten that it had occurred. There was a big picture of me at the head of the table, surrounded by my oil field Shriner buddies. My girls thought that it was great and told me how proud of me they were. "You always took care of us, Dad, and we remember everything you did."

"Good," I said, "because I sure as hell don't."

The next morning, I got up and took the first bus out of Irvine, heading north to Los Angeles. When I got there, I transferred to an express bus heading north to Eugene. When I got there, I went next door to a bar called Diablo's Downtown Lodge. When I entered it, my editor happened to be sitting there.

He asked me how my trip was, and I told him it was a disaster. "It's all in my notes," I said. "I did what I could but it was pretty horrible."

"Well, did you get to see Greg?" he asked.

"I did."

"Well then, what was such a disaster about it?"

"Come out to Florence next week and I'll tell you all about it."

When I got home, I looked at my notes and made some more comments about what had happened in Ensenada. About a week later, when my editor came out, I gave him the notes and told him what had happened, that I thought I had learned nothing. Later in the week, after we talked more about it, I found out that I was wrong. When he left later that week I began looking over the notes that we made together and saw the missing pieces that would complete the jigsaw puzzle of my life and times and how it all fit together.

Six
Last Notes from Florence

My entire life began and will end in Florence. It seems like that it's just one long street that has stuck with me my whole life. I was born in Mission Hospital, on Florence Boulevard in Los Angeles, grew up in that house in the Florence section of L.A. on 69th and Converse Streets, and now live in a trailer park in Florence, Oregon. And when I die here, sometime in the not too distant future, my buddies from the Florence Moose Lodge will take my ashes and sprinkle them in the Ten Mile River just north of town up near the lovely town of Yachats.

The only times I've been away from one Florence or another was during my time in the Navy in the South Pacific, my years working in the oil fields, and the time that I spent with my fourth wife, BB, in Utah and Nevada. The only other exception to it is the time I spent with The Redhead.

Now, as I'm looking back on it and filling in a hole or two with what little memory I have left, it's beginning to make a bit more sense to me. I say beginning, because it's still coming back, most of it in dribs and drabs, in partial recollections, in names and places remembered.

When I began this book, my editor told me that it was going to test me in ways that I hadn't expected and that it would bring up a lot of things that I might not like. He was right; by the end of the month of July when I was getting close to finishing it, I was beginning to wear out. It brought up a lot of memories, some of them good, many of them bad. And it brought up a lot of bitterness, mostly from the memories of The Redhead.

There are no photos that I have of my mother; no letters either. When I think back on her, it always brings up something foul and painful. She was not a nice woman. Nobody could understand her—not her mother, not me, not Hank Messler, not his mother, not anybody as far as I knew.

So far as I can see it, Ila Ona "Peggy" Baker was pretty much a nymphomaniac, as far as I understand that term. She enjoyed hurting people. She enjoyed the physical company of men who she'd use like a dishrag and then toss away when a better one came along. She dumped her own son on a Mexican family that she didn't really know, then kidnapped him from his grandparents, then beat him with welding irons and frying pans, then stuck him with knives, then destroyed his soap box derby racer, then lied to him and robbed him, and verbally abused him on a daily basis. How can you understand somebody like that? I certainly can't, even though I've tried. The best that I can come up with is that she was sick—mentally and emotionally sick, maybe a psycho.

In my adult years, I asked myself what in the hell ever possessed her to behave like she did? I kept thinking that I was somehow at fault; that I had done something to bring on her brutal behavior. All that I have left from her are the memories, the emotional scars, and the words of others who called her everything from "nutty" to "slutty." I do know that in these days she would have never gotten away with treating a child the way that she did—not with the strict child abuse laws that are on the books today.

The way I see it, she didn't deserve to have a child, and when I think about that it really gets painful, because then I wouldn't be here either, would I?

When I talk with some people or watch some programs on television dealing with females who have similar traits with The Redhead, they often say that somebody like Ila Ona Baker must have suffered from some kind of child abuse herself. I know that my editor does; he thinks she was probably sexually molested by a man in her family—a brother, and uncle or cousin; maybe her father. Maybe it's true, but it still doesn't lessen the hurt or the bitterness that I've carried towards her for sixty years now.

As far as my mother is concerned, I have no idea of what it was that happened to her to turn her into the kind of person she was. And now there is probably nobody left on the planet that could answer that. The last time I saw her was at Grandpa's funeral, and that was fifty years ago.

I am wondering if I'll be able to forgive her, and right now as I write this, I don't think I can. Maybe it's not very wise to carry this kind of bitterness into the grave, but it seems I probably will. I just can't think of something that will change this. I just don't see it.

There is maybe some irony to the fact that I was able to live a relatively normal life after all of the wild shit that I went through from birth to sixteen years old. I've been married four times, two of them successfully, one of them horrible, and one that barely lasted six months before we had it annulled. I have three lovely girls who love and respect me and they're all successful. I have six grandchildren as well.

I served in the Navy with the Seabees during World War II, and was honorably discharged after it ended. We were in the Marshalls, the Marianas, Okinawa, Guam, Saipan, Anawetok, Midway, the Kwajeleins, Truk, and other islands without names, fighting fascism as represented by the Japs, a word that you're not supposed to use anymore. The only ones who do use it are people from my generation, and we're a dying breed, I know that. I fought battles against them on those islands, and saw a friend of mine get his head blown off which landed in my lap while my friend still stood there firing like Roland the Headless Thompson Gunner, or so the song goes anyway. It was a horrendous sight. I worked from when I was a kid until I retired in 1983. I worked on oilfields in Iraq and Kuwait and Afghanistan where the war on terrorism is now blazing; in India and Hong Kong and the Dutch Indies and Australia; in England and Germany and Northern Spain and the Canary Islands, where the Velascos sailed from to the New World. Then, when I retired from all that, I then spent much of my time managing properties in Utah and Lake Mead, Nevada with BB, and those were good years for me. I had finally found a woman whom I loved and could trust. She was the love of my life and I think I'll be joining her soon. I hope so, I miss her every day.

In the three weeks since I got home to Florence from my time in Ensenada, I've read these pages again and again and tried as best I could to fill in the gaps that were missing. Some things did surface, but not that much, and pretty soon I was back at my old routine of going to the library, The Moose Club, grocery shopping and doctors.

At the beginning of August my editor called me and said he was coming out to see me. I asked him why, since the book was pretty much finished and that I didn't want to go through any more of it. He asked me if I wanted to finish it, and I said that I did. "I thought it's done," I told him. "Almost," was his reply.

When he came out to see me he said that we still had a few things left to deal with. “Like what?” I asked. He handed me a few pages with questions on them and then he left a few minutes later after I’d read them. “Send me the answers as soon as you can, Russ. Then we’re finished.”

I looked at the questions for a few days. I thought some of what he wanted was bullshit and called him up and read him the riot act. He told me to look at them again and tell him what I could. Then I started taping what he asked me for. There were a few questions that got under my skin and I wanted to answer them as fully and honestly as I could.

I didn’t realize how much that writing this book would take out of me and sometimes I ask myself why I even bothered to do it. When my editor was here I told him “I didn’t really want to write this book,” and he asked me “Then why do I happen to be sitting here? I wouldn’t be here unless you made the decision to write it, would I?”

He had me on that point. He was right. There must have been some reason that I made a decision to take this on and so I began to think about why that was.

In some way I felt that this book was pushed on me by other people. They’d hear my stories down at The Moose or other places and say that I ought to write a book about them. They’d tell me that I’d lived a life that was worth writing about, and now I see that *maybe* they were right.

How does this kid from Florence survive a strict religious upbringing followed by child abuse and cruelty and somehow manage to lead a decent life? In some ways, I guess the reason that I did write this book was to better understand myself. I have come to see how important it was for me to have people like Grandpa and Hank Messler and Uncle Clint in my life, because they showed me kindness and respect and it carried over into my adult life.

I also think that I wrote this book because I thought it might help others as well, especially those who have gone through similar hard times like I did with The Redhead. I hope that it gives them some strength and understanding, and even some enjoyment. You can survive unspeakable horrors and live to tell the tale if you can reach down inside yourself and draw strength from others who will help you, either directly or by example.

I don't know if the book has changed me that much. It brought up a lot of bitterness and a lot of memories of things that I thought I had long forgotten, and I do think that it did help me reconnect to my kids in a stronger way. At one point in my life, from the early 1950s until the early 1990s I didn't even see my three girls. I was on the road with the oil and truck companies; I was still hurting from the memory of their mother and the breakup of our marriage. But then, when I saw them again at a big reunion that we held at an Italian restaurant, we patched things up and now we talk all the time and visit one another whenever we can.

I've thought sometimes about the only other Florence that I haven't been to yet, the one in Italy, where the Renaissance began. My editor says that it's a beautiful place and that I should see it before I die. He tells me stories about it and says it's one of the most beautiful cities on earth.

I never did spend much time in Europe and maybe I should have gone there with BB when she was alive. Although I would like to go there and see the only Florence that I missed, I think I'm too sick now and wouldn't be able to enjoy it like I would have when I was young. That's one place I've missed; and maybe one thing I regret.

In the days that are still left to me I look forward to the visits with my kids, and to the visits of my friends like Fred and Kathy and other friends from my oil and trucking days who come up here to Florence. We take trips up the coast, hang out at the Moose and have a few drinks, go camping in r.v.'s, talk about old times, good times.

Let me be perfectly clear here: I do know that I'm dying and there's nothing that's going to save me short of a miracle. Do I believe in miracles? I tell myself no, that I don't. But I do remember the miracle that saved my arm. And I do remember the miracle that saved my life, when Papa took me in when I was a baby and saved me from probable infant abuse at the hands of The Redhead. Who knows? Maybe I've still got one miracle left.

One of the questions on that sheet of paper that my editor left me asked if I believed in an afterlife, did I believe in God, and was there anything left of us after our physical bodies were gone.

Those are hard questions for me because Grandma pretty well ruined me on religion and other matters of spirituality. I think I can honestly say that I don't believe in God—not in the way that most people do. I sometimes look into the sky and say "OK, sonofabitch, what've you got for me now? What kind of shit am I going to have to go through today?"

I think that God is dead, and so far as I can see he's been that way ever since I was born. I don't think there's an afterlife. What I believe in is that when your physical life is over, then that's the end of you. It might be a cold thing to say, but that's how I feel.

I think that I'll probably just spend the rest of my life around here in Florence, Oregon; I don't think that I want to go into some nursing home if things keep getting worse for me. If I keep going downhill, I'll just go down to the

Moose one day, have a few more brandy and Cokes than usual, and then come home and end it all with my rifle. What that will mean, I really can't say, but the idea of being a vegetable isn't something that appeals to me. Life is difficult for me now and it's better for me to just sit here and let death come, hopefully without too much pain.

I know that's a kind of mournful note, and though it's possible I don't spend too much time dwelling on that. I go through my manuscript, editing as I go, and send the pages back and forth to Eugene. I get up every day and watch the news and try to remain informed about current affairs. I talk to my kids and my friends and my doctors.

So here I sit with the days winding down to dust. I'm Claude M. Russell of many Florences and two countries and at least one book. I know more now about myself and the people in my life than I did at the beginning. If a miracle happens and I'm somehow restored to health, then maybe I'll see that other Florence. If not, I'll soon be joining BB and Papa. I know that he said that he'd be holding the furnace door open for me, but I'm hoping that he's wrong and I'll be heading elsewhere, because I sure know that if such places exist, that The Redhead will likely be there inside the furnace. I think it's safe to say that another reunion with her would be none too pleasant. The first was more than enough, and I'm happy that the last words that I write in this book are these: I lived to tell the tale.